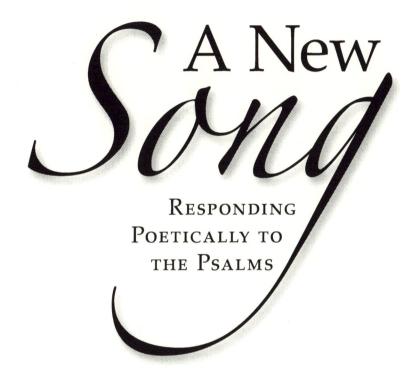

A New Song

Responding Poetically to the Psalms

D. P. Myers

WestBow Press
A DIVISION OF THOMAS NELSON
& ZONDERVAN

Copyright © 2016 D. P. Myers.

All rights reserved. No part of this book may be used or reproduced by any means, graphic, electronic, or mechanical, including photocopying, recording, taping or by any information storage retrieval system without the written permission of the author except in the case of brief quotations embodied in critical articles and reviews.

Scripture quotations are from The Holy Bible, English Standard Version® (ESV®), copyright © 2001 by Crossway, a publishing ministry of Good News Publishers. Used by permission. All rights reserved.

This book is a work of non-fiction. Unless otherwise noted, the author and the publisher make no explicit guarantees as to the accuracy of the information contained in this book and in some cases, names of people and places have been altered to protect their privacy.

WestBow Press books may be ordered through booksellers or by contacting:

WestBow Press
A Division of Thomas Nelson & Zondervan
1663 Liberty Drive
Bloomington, IN 47403
www.westbowpress.com
1 (866) 928-1240

Because of the dynamic nature of the Internet, any web addresses or links contained in this book may have changed since publication and may no longer be valid. The views expressed in this work are solely those of the author and do not necessarily reflect the views of the publisher, and the publisher hereby disclaims any responsibility for them.

Any people depicted in stock imagery provided by Thinkstock are models, and such images are being used for illustrative purposes only. Certain stock imagery © Thinkstock.

ISBN: 978-1-5127-4171-1 (sc)
ISBN: 978-1-5127-4172-8 (hc)
ISBN: 978-1-5127-4170-4 (e)

Library of Congress Control Number: 2016907818

Print information available on the last page.

WestBow Press rev. date: 06/10/2016

To George MacDonald, one of my many mentors,
living and dead, from whom I have learned so much
and from whom I have yet much to learn.

My prayer-bird was cold—would not away,
Although I set it on the edge of the nest.
Then I bethought me of the story old—
Love-fact or loving fable, thou know'st best—
How, when the children had made sparrows of clay,
Thou mad'st them birds, with wings to flutter and fold:
Take, Lord, my prayer in thy hand, and make it pray.

My poor clay sparrow seems turned to a stone,
And from my heart will neither fly nor run.
I cannot feel as thou and I both would,
But, Father, I am willing—make me good.
What art thou Father for, but to help thy son?
Look deep, yet deeper, in my heart, and there,
Beyond where I can feel, read thou the prayer.

—George MacDonald, *Diary of an Old Soul*

Contents

Acknowledgments xi
Introduction xiii
Chapter 1: My Question 1
Chapter 2: Struggles, Scripture, and Creativity 3
Chapter 3: Poetic Responses to the Psalms 13
    Responses to Book One of the Psalms: 1 – 41 13
    Responses to Book Two of the Psalms: 42 – 72 57
    Responses to Book Three of the Psalms: 73 – 89 92
    Responses to Book Four of the Psalms: 90 – 106 110
    Responses to Book Five of the Psalms: 107 – 150 131
Chapter 4: Creative Ways to Respond to God's Word 198
Chapter 5: Final Thoughts: A New Song 207
Bibliography 211

Acknowledgments

> No man is an *Iland*, intire of it selfe; every man is a peece of the *Continent*, a part of the *maine*.
>
> —John Donne, Meditation XVII in
> *Devotions upon Emergent Occasions*

Thanks to Dr. Rob Price, who first allowed me to investigate poetic responses to the Psalms.

Thanks to Dr. Ken Way, who helped to excite in me a love for the wisdom literature of Scripture and allowed great latitude for my research paper in his Old Testament class, which was, to a certain degree, a formative influence on this current work.

Thanks to Leroy Case and L. T. Newland for their friendship and encouraging feedback on the poetry with which I frequently filled their in-boxes.

Thanks to Alexandra Repke and Elizabeth Emerson for their support and willingness to offer honest critiques.

Thanks to Steve Baarendse for a friendship that reaches back to college, the likes of which I wish everyone might experience, and for his thoughtful comments on the prose portions of this book.

And finally, a special thanks to Ami Wagner for her friendship and willingness to offer meaningful critiques, all of which have helped to make this book better than it would have been without her insight.

Introduction

Over the years I have had a number of conversations with fellow believers confirming my experience: devotions can often become tiresome and difficult to sustain. While there are likely those who have rarely or never struggled with their motivation to read Scripture, find something of interest in the text, or pray, I'm not one of those people. Rather I've found that my desire for devotional reading of Scripture has often been like "a wave of the sea that is driven and tossed by the wind" (James 1:6). It is true there have been times when being in the Word was a highly anticipated event but it is more frequent for me to be lazy and unmotivated, going for days, weeks, or even longer without opening the Bible except for Sundays at church.

In addition to this fluctuating desire for the Scriptures, there have been times when I've wondered if my approach to reading Scripture was improperly motivated. What I mean is that I've found that I can easily fall in love with words, structures, stories, and the greater narrative of the text but forget the fact that Scripture is a only a sign pointing to a greater reality—the person of Jesus. In these times I feel like I'm one of the people to whom Jesus spoke in John 5:39–40 when he said, "You search the Scriptures because you think that in them you have eternal life; and it is they that bear witness about me, yet you refuse to come to me that you may have life." Essentially, my eyes would rarely look *through* the Scripture to see Jesus; rather, they looked *at* the Scriptures and saw words.

Even with these struggles, I know that if I'm to continue growing spiritually, I need to read the Bible consistently. Yet I often find myself trudging through the text verse by verse only to realize after a few minutes that my mind is elsewhere, reviewing the upcoming day's schedule, replaying highlights of the movie or sporting event I saw the night before, or indulging in any one of the almost infinite number of possible distractions

I can easily find. At such times I usually end up reading the passage three or four times before realizing I have no idea what the passage is saying. I then often just give up, close the Bible, say a prayer, and go on with my day.

Unless I miss my mark, I think this struggle occurs more frequently than most people would like to admit, leaving well-meaning believers in a dry time with regard to reading the Bible. While I don't think there is a magic pill to solve this problem, it's possible that as we see how others approach their devotional time, we can learn new things that may help with our own struggles. It's with this assumption in mind that I present this book. Our specific struggles may not be the same, but I hope that as you read how I've approached the reading of Scripture—and in particular the book of Psalms—you may be encouraged to once again open the Bible with fresh eyes to see what the Lord might have for you to learn about him and about yourself.

Chapter 1
My Question

Why am I always thinking
    you judge my doubts and fears
When questions are so many
    from those you hold so dear?

David, Korah, Solomon,
    Asaph, and Moses, too,
Called out with many questions
    directed unto you.

From deep pain and lonely days
    and times they thought you fled
To breath 'fore their earthen graves
    where last each lay their head,

All these men held on to you
    through stages of their lives
Yet questioned what you're doing
    with love through life's long strife.

I'm sure they weren't all perfect
    and living without sin,
Yet in your steadfast loving,
    you cleansed them from within.

D. P. Myers

So can I look unto them
    to guide me through each day?
And will you still take questions
    from me along life's way?

Just as you have led them all
    with steady and sure hand,
Will you move me onward now
    and to your holy land?

Lord, help me in my questions
    to know your steadfast love,
A love that guides this blind man
    with sure hand from above.

Chapter 2
Struggles, Scripture, and Creativity

A few years ago, I went through a particularly difficult personal time. I had just returned to school after a holiday break, and in my loneliness I was confronted anew with my sinful nature. But this wasn't the typical momentary struggle that so often can be forgotten in the morning after a good night's sleep. No, this turned into a depression that overwhelmed my life for a number of weeks. I didn't sleep well. I could barely maintain focus on those things that I needed to do for class, and I felt disconnected and empty when going to Scripture.

During this dark time, I prayed in much the same way that I had done numerous times before that the Lord would "take this thorn from me" (2 Corinthians 12:8). While I know Scripture indicates that Paul only issued his request three times, I guess I'm a bit stubborn and slow to get the message because over the course of my life I've offered this petition numerous times—most certainly more than three. Needless to say, as with all the previous times, my request was not granted, and my struggles persisted. I got very little sleep and gave little quality attention to my schoolwork, and my time with God suffered greatly.

I had no idea where to go in Scripture, so by this point I was jumping around the Bible, looking for some passage that might possibly speak truth and encouragement to me. I started in the Epistles and then moved to the Gospels. Not satisfied, I then went to the history books of the Old Testament and finally to the Prophets. But nothing provided any peace. I was at a loss and about to give up for good, but then I decided to read through the Psalms. I used to think that reading the book of Psalms was a sort of cop-out, but since nothing else in Scripture seemed to alleviate the ache, I decided to read one psalm a day as a sort of last resort.

It wasn't long before I was doing more than just reading a psalm each day. I read and reread the psalm a number of times each day and found myself easily lost in meditation. I was connecting with them in ways I hadn't before, and it wasn't long before reading and meditation turned into prayer. At first these prayers were merely repetition of the themes in the psalms, but the prayers soon shifted focus to areas of my life needing to be addressed. These areas were often things that I was struggling with at the time and at other times things I felt but had never been able to verbalize. At other times I was confronted with issues in my past that I had not ever fully dealt with.

This pattern of reading, prayer, and meditation continued for quite some time. Each day I would lie on a spot on the floor and have the Bible in front of me. Leaning on my elbows, I would read the psalm a few times and then lie face down, meditating and praying. Many days I was moved to tears, and at times I felt like I was in the presence of God. On other days I felt alone and in a vacuum. Regardless of the experience I had each day, I chose to continue the habit of reading, meditating, and praying through the Psalms. Even when a school project was pressing or a test was around the corner, I kept my appointment with God on the floor and in the Bible.

• • •

On the surface, what I've just described is not much different from many of my previous efforts. But another thing was happening in my life during this time; I was becoming more interested in the arts and the human creative impulse. This interest was not new, for as long as I can remember, I've enjoyed the arts even though I've frequently felt a tension between the arts and the seemingly rigid doctrinal compartments of Christianity. What I mean is that on the one hand, I was very comfortable with logic and reason, even teaching apologetics for a number of years in a Christian high school. But on the other hand, I always felt that a solely rational approach to Scripture was disconnected from my experience. Logic, reason, and proper exegesis of Scripture helped me understand God in a way that I could love him with mind, but my heart often felt untouched.

Absolute, unchanging, and divine truth is one thing, but human experience is another. Emotions, angst, turmoil, and joy—these things were often left out of my theology. This disconnect was felt in my heart and at the edges of my mind, but I could never put a finger on its root cause. But through the writings of George MacDonald, C. S. Lewis, J. R. R. Tolkien, Dorothy Sayers, and others on creativity, imagination, fantasy, and the arts, I started to understand this tension. It was Dorothy Sayers's work *The Mind of the Maker* that helped me the most. She builds her premise from the observation that the primary thing to know about God by the time man was declared to be made in his image in Genesis 1:27 is that he is a creator. And thus, for her it seems to follow that at least part of what being made in God's image means is that we are creative as well. We do not *choose* to be creative. Rather we *are* creative.

It's true that Scripture has much more to say about the *imago Dei*, but we would be remiss if we didn't pay attention to Sayers's conclusion. God is a creator, and thus, so are we. But it's important to note that there's one major difference between God's creativity and our own. He creates from nothing while we require preexistent reality before we can create. God brought forth the universe from nothing, but the first act of human creativity in Genesis 2 is when God placed man in the garden with the beasts that he had created and then told Adam to name them all. The text says, "Now out of the ground the Lord God had formed every beast of the field and every bird of the heavens and brought them to the man *to see what he would call them*. And whatever the man called every living creature, that was its name" (Genesis 2:19, emphasis added). It's interesting to note that after creating the universe and after giving man the capacity for language, God then *expectantly waited to see what names man would create* for the animals in the world around him. Could it then also be true that God expectantly waits to see what each of us will create as a result of our response to him, his word, and his created world surrounding us?

• • •

These thoughts about the creative impulse were running through my mind at the same time I was working through the Psalms for a second time. Not being well versed in how to respond creatively, I began by writing some basic one-line responses to the text. These weren't journal responses discussing my feelings about the text, lessons learned, or applications. They were just responses, often the first thing coming to mind after reading the text. The first psalm that I wrote anything for was Psalm 42, and I simply wrote the question, "Why do I allow my melancholy to overcome God's mercies?" The next day after reading Psalm 43, I wrote a sort of prayer list that said, "That I would hope for God and praise him again. Eyes to see your work and hand in and behind the realities of the day. Your truth to enlighten my mind and enliven my heart."

It wasn't long, however, before my responses turned into short poem-like musings. One of the first was written in response to Psalm 55.

> How can I cry for justice
> When I long for mercy
> How can I pray for enemies
>   Meet their just end
> When I seek to live
>   In the house of God
> I must love my enemy
>   as I love myself
> I must cry for mercy
>   for them in their sin
> Or I must embrace the
>   hand of God's wrath
> In my life and in theirs
> For my heart of sin
> Is brother to my enemies

This continued as I read through the book of Psalms each day, and I found a connection with the Word of God that I had not known in years ... or maybe ever. Instead of reading a passage of Scripture and asking what I could get out of it, I allowed the material given by God—in this case the Psalms—to filter through my mind and heart before considering a response. Devotional time, which had previously been a means to know more rationally about God, soon became a much more personal time.

I suppose this may seem very much like a subtle variation of journaling; however, I have done that in the past, and at least for me, this process was a different experience. My journals in the past were primarily centered on how I felt and thought about the text, focusing on some sort of application to my immediate circumstance. But as I wrote poems, I found two things to be quite different. First, these interactions were less focused on my experience and more focused on God and His work. It's certainly true that my experience molded the words of the poems, but I found the poetry was a way of looking elsewhere, specifically to his throne. The second major difference was that, unlike a personal journal, when I wrote a poem, I was using a creative voice that I had rarely exercised in the past. I can't help but think that in using this creative voice, God waited like he did for Adam in anticipation and was pleased with my creative product. I was taking what he had given me, namely his Word and my voice, and returned it to him with my own element of creativity attached to it. In fact, I think this may be what the psalmists mean when they urge us to sing a new song.

Until recently, however, I had assumed that the new songs to be sung were either the Psalms themselves or what those who are skilled at writing music and lyrics have penned for us to sing. From both sources we have a rich tradition of worship songs to draw from, especially for those of us who are not so talented at composition. But I don't think that the Lord only wants us to repeat the words of others; I think he's pleased when we sing to him *our* new song. And while we might not have the insight or talent found in the historical and modern songwriters, their songs are not always our songs. It is this thought that George MacDonald echoes in *Unspoken Sermons I: The New Name* where he says, "This or that man may understand God more, may understand God better than he, but no other man can understand God as he understands him." Essentially, MacDonald says that each of us has a unique way of understanding God that does not overlap with what others know of God. MacDonald continues,

> There is a chamber also—(O God, humble and accept my speech)—a chamber in God Himself, into which none can enter but the one, the individual, the peculiar man,—out of which chamber that man has to bring revelation and strength for his brethren. That is that for which he was made—to reveal the secret things of the Father.

We were created by God to share our unique experience of God with others in the body of Christ.

Each of us has God-given creative talents that help us form and sing our own new song. Some of us have the ability to write poetry, some to paint pictures or take photographs, others to sculpt, tell stories, or write plays and essays. Each of us—yes, each and every one of us—has been given a unique voice with a unique creative language by which we sing a new song about God ... to God and to others, which is our own form of creative worship. But only if we use these talents to respond to God's Word and his world will our new songs help others come into the presence of the infinite. Thus, not only is our individual time of worship with its creative response enriching to ourselves, but others can also find their experience with God (and augment that experience) as we share our new songs with them.

However, the idea of sharing my experience with others brought with it fear. With so many talented artists in the world, so many talented preachers and expositors, I often doubt that anything I could say would be of benefit to others. Even more, as I think about my own creative impulse, I'm quickly burdened with the desire to produce something of excellence, which is often defined by comparison. For instance, when I played soccer, I always knew who the best player on the field was and knew I could never be him. When I was on stage, it was not difficult to identify the most talented individual, someone I rarely was. And when it comes to writing, I realize that the genius of the great authors is beyond my capacity. The reality is that I will most likely never be the best at anything. And it's not just me. Most of us are (and will always be) average. That is the statistical nature of reality. But that should not stop any one of us from creating. The fact of the matter is that I think God expects us to respond creatively to him even if we are average. I don't think we are supposed to compare our works and words with others. I think we're supposed to sing our new song and allow the Lord to do the rest. It was two of Christ's parables that helped me understand this fact.

The first is the story of the widow's offering found in Mark and Luke's gospel. Jesus, seeing a small offering given by a poor widow surrounded by rich people contributing large sums of money, said, "This poor widow has put in more than all of them. For they all contributed out of their abundance, but she out of her poverty put in all she had to live on" (Luke 21:3–4). The Lord sees our offerings, no matter how small and seemingly insignificant, in light of what it is we have to give, not in comparison to the wealth of others. And so while Mozart, Rembrandt, Milton, Bernini, Shakespeare, Einstein, Faraday, Curie, Hawking, and others might be seen as masters in their fields, that is no guarantee that God values their offerings more highly than the poem written or picture drawn by any one of us. When we genuinely offer up to him a new song of worship out of our poverty, the Lord accepts it as a fragrant offering, acceptable and pleasing to Him. Of course, this doesn't mean that what we offer is valued highly enough by human standards to be marketed and sold to the masses, but it does mean that our offering is highly valued by God's standards, a valuation that is far more important than any human measure.

While the story of the widow's mite helped me understand that God values all contribution, it is the parable of the talents in Matthew and Luke that compelled me to act. The parable of the talents tells of a rich man giving some servants various amounts of money before leaving on a journey. Upon his return, he finds that some of the servants had increased the wealth given them by various percentages. With these servants the master was pleased *regardless* of the percentage increase that they had achieved. But there was one servant who was so afraid of losing what had been entrusted to him that he had hid the money in the ground. When the rich man returned, he gave back the exact amount of money that was given to him. But as you might remember, the rich man was not at all pleased with this fearful servant. The rich man took the money from the fearful servant, gave it to the one who had the greatest return, and then cast the fearful man out of his presence.

God does not merely hope that we take the talents he has given us and do something with them. *He expects it.* If our talents are as small as the widow's mite, he wants them offered to him. If our talent is as world-renowned as Beethoven's or Rembrandt's, he wants it offered to him. But in either case, if we fearfully hold on to our talent and bury it so that no one receives a benefit, then we should know that God is displeased with us and it is possible that his wrath will be poured out on us at some point. I realize that these are hard words with strong implications, but I think that God is serious about his call on our lives. And if the *Westminster Catechism* is right that "man's chief end is to glorify God, and to enjoy him for ever," then part of what it means to glorify God is to sing his praises, the very thing that creating a new song is all about.

• • •

It is with these things in mind that I compiled this volume of poetry. It came as a result of my encounters with God while reading, meditating on, and praying through the Psalms. While reading these poems may be a devotional experience for some—and I hope it is—that was not my primary purpose in writing and compiling it. First of all, it was a record of my personal experience with God through his book of Psalms. This collection will always be to me something that it cannot be for others—a road map showing me glimpses of the path my life has taken. Even now when I reread some poems, I am reminded of the place I was and how much God has helped me since writing them. In others, I find that I am still struggling through the same battles, and in a few instances, I seem to have spiritually regressed. Thus, for me this book will always be a personal collection in a way that others can and will never know.

Yet even so, I don't mean to say that others can't learn from reading these poems. In fact, the second purpose for this compilation is that if others would someday read these poems, there might be a chance they could glimpse McDonald's "chamber in God Himself" I have glimpsed. This does not mean that my insights are necessarily unique. In fact, it's quite possible that many of these poems may reflect what others have already seen of God. And in many instances, others may be able to state what I have seen and felt in a much better way than I have. But—and this is the important point—these words came from my experience with God and are told through my own voice, and as such, they may help others know that they are not alone in their struggle through life. In *Shadowlands*, a movie about the life of C. S. Lewis with Joy Davidman, Lewis encounters one of his students on a train. In the course of the conversation, the student says, "We read to know we're not alone." In like manner, if somehow you read these poems and find that your experience with God, though unique to you, is like the experiences that others are having, then this book of poetry will have served its second purpose.

But as important as it might be to record my personal experiences with God and to share them so as to help others find comfort in their journeys, it's the third purpose for this book that I think may be the most important. In the introduction to the first edition of George MacDonald's book *A Book of Strife in the Form of the Diary of an Old Soul*, published in 1880, a book we now know as *Diary of an Old Soul*, MacDonald writes,

> Sweet friends, receive my offering. You will find
> Against each worded page a white page set:—
> This is the mirror of each friendly mind

> Reflecting that. In this book we are met.
> Make it, dear hearts, of worth to you indeed:—
> Let your white page be ground, my print be seed,
> Growing to golden ears, that faith and hope shall feed.

When the first edition of the book was initially printed, he had his poems written only on the left side page of the book, leaving the right side page blank. He did this to leave space for his readers to record any thoughtful responses they might have while reading his work. While I'm not expecting that you respond to my words, it is my hope that you might see in my work an example of how you might creatively respond to God's Word.[1] Like me, you may be prompted to respond to Scripture through poetry as your new song of worship. But not all of us respond to God with a poetic voice. You might be a painter. Then consider placing your new song on a canvas. You might be a dancer. Then dance as David did before the Lord. You might sculpt, draw, write, or compose music. Form your new song in whatever medium best suits your voice.

I am convinced that each of us has a creative voice that speaks in the realm of the arts, but it is important to realize that creativity is not solely limited to the arts. Some extremely creative people are immersed in the study of mathematics, physics, biology, management, or economics. In fact, if we look carefully at Genesis 2:19, the first record of human creativity, we find it to be one of biology, a work in the realm of science, not the arts. As such, even though this current work focuses on a creative *artistic* response to God's Word, we must not think that the arts are the sole gatekeepers of creativity. Nor must we think that the artistic creative voice is the only new song that we can sing to God.

However you choose to exercise your creative voice I would be remiss if I didn't state one major caution. Given the world in which we live today where people elevate personal experience beyond its proper status, we must remember that our creative voice is a *response* to God's work, his Word, and the movement of his Spirit and his person. It is never a *substitute* for God's Word, Spirit, or person. This isn't to deny the importance of the many deeply moving and awe-inspiring works of art that have been

---

[1] If you would like to read other's poetic responses to the Psalms, I recommend the twenty-one sonnets of Anne Lock, written as a meditation on Psalm 51 in the 1500s. References to her work can be found in the bibliography.

created in response to the world around us with all of its pain, pleasures, beauty, and ugliness. Such works are necessary, and in many cases they are divinely influenced acts of creativity to which we need to heed. But when we approach God to hear his voice and form our new song in the context of personal spiritual growth, I believe we must start with the Word, work, and person of God. We must pray with George MacDonald, "Fill us with the words that proceed out of thy mouth." And it is not just MacDonald who holds such a view. Even the artist Vincent van Gogh understood this in his early years. On May 19, 1877, he wrote his brother Theo and said,

> For one's own work, thoughts and observations are not enough, we need the comfort and blessing and guidance of a higher power, and that is something anyone who is at all serious and who longs to lift up his soul to the light is sure to recognize and experience. Pining for God works like leaven on dough. May it also prove to be true in the story of both our lives.

Immersion in the Word—and the ensuing study, meditation, and prayer—prepares our voices of worship so that we can respond in a pleasing manner to God. God waits to hear how we'll respond to what he has provided. His living Word makes dead men live again to sing his praise. I would encourage you to allow the Spirit to free your creative voice as you respond to his Word with a new song of worship that can only come from you.

Chapter 3
Poetic Responses to the Psalms

Responses to Book One[2] of the Psalms: 1 – 41

1[3]

Like a tree you plant the ones
    Who love your truth and laws.
Like the chaff in wind's swift run
    The wicked soon withdraws.

Root that drinks from living stream
    Brings life to leaf and fruit.
Such the righteous it would seem
    Whose way you don't refute.

---

[2] I have retained the five book designations found in The Psalms to segment this chapter of poetry. While there was not a conscious effort by me to restrict the content of each poem to the predominate themes found in each of the five books, I chose to maintain the given structure of the Psalms here out of deference to Scripture.
[3] Each poem's designation number corresponds to the same Psalm in The Psalms.

D. P. Myers

Saplings by the holy flow
    Are not the only trees.
Readers of your story know
    A hewn tree was for thee.

But fruit plucked in garden fair
    And tasted by the tongue
Drove us out from when and where
    Your voice had clearly rung.

From that time we all have roamed
    Round earth so dark and cold;
With fallen souls we have combed
    All lands for truth of old.

Never have we found such hints
    In earth's broad sweeping land
As we found on stony prints
    Engraved by holy hand.

Words impressed on tables hard
    Become for sons of God
Living and a holy guard
    For narrow ways not broad.

But such guards will sin not cure
    For that we need some blood
Flowing down a hewn tree sure
    A wash by holy flood.

Graven stone and living word
    Will prosper righteous man
But more is there to be heard
    Of trees within God's plan.

A New Song

Righteous men and evil strife
    Will war through ages long
Until end of earthly life
    And one tree still stands strong.

Tree of Life and water clear
    That flows from holy throne,
Monthly fruit for every tear
    That man has ever known.

Till that distant future day
    His law is my delight
Through it God will light my way
    And give to me clear sight;

As is found in start and end
    With God's trees standing tall
In the midst the word God sends
    Makes righteous trees of all.

2

Why must I be afraid of thee?
    Why must I ever cry?
Why is there wrath in your path?
    Why does my fear not die?

Over the earth you laugh in mirth.
    Over all kings you sing.
Wars your strong son has 'ready won
    Victory do you bring.

Why do we fight your holy light?
    Why do we rage in vain?
Why do we battle you who's true?
    Why must bent knee need pain?

D. P. Myers

3

Can I, Lord, exceed your grace?
    Can I step beyond?
Is no longer there a place
    With you that I am found?

Foes I have surrounding me
    Some of them I've known.
All are saying that with thee
    I am no longer home.

Exiled from your Promised Land
    Quickly I'm pushed out.
Is this movement from your hand?
    My heart still lives in doubt.

Sins of mine I know too well,
    Breaking moral law.
How I want your voice to yell
    And judge my every flaw.

Rest instead you often give
    After evil day.
Showing me how that I'll live
    Long in your holy way.

David ran from jealous son,
    Wanting to be king,
But you know I also run
    Away from loving wing.

Like on mount you gave to him
    Food from servants yours,
Now to me your love does brim
    And over me it pours.

Someday soon, I know not when,
    Justice will stand tall.
But until such time as then,
    In faith I pledge my all.

4

Late at night with curtains drawn
When head upon my pillow falls
Open eyes and with no yawn
I ponder constant shameful calls;

Calls from men who laugh at me
And seek my joyful life to end
And from words that I'm not free
The lies of theirs I can't defend.

In such times I call to you
And wonder why these men hold sway
Over life once given to
Your word and people ev'ry day.

Late at night in bed I fret
About my life so empty now.
In the silence there I set
Aside my dreams and wonder how

You in heaven high above
Work your plan through exile mine
And to all convey your love
And show the righteousness of thine.

In the silent dark you speak
And tell me in your ways I must
Douse my pride and then be meek
And ever in your plan to trust.

D. P. Myers

Help me in the angst I know
Your peace receive and laws to keep,
And to the dying world show
That in your loving arms I'll sleep.

5

Wicked ones near and far
    Draw me to the night.
From, O Lord, where you are
    Pull me to the light.

Thus, my cry comes to you
    In the morning's dawn
When the grass wet with dew
    Lights my deepest song:

Keep me from evil ways
    Make my path go straight.
Comfort me all my days
    Take my sinful weight.

Let me bow at your throne
    Cover me with love.
Hear my heart's crying tone
    Offered you above.

6

Oftentimes I pray and cry
And ask you, Lord, Why? Oh, why?
Often lips with mournful song
Ask of you, How long, how long?
Late at night in tears I lay
Wond'ring why you went away.
Years ago I used to hear
Your clear voice to me so near.
Long ago I used to know
Where you guided me to go.
But of late on bed of pain
Tears fall freely like the rain.
Empty heart cries out so loud.
Lonely soul stands in the crowd.
Where and what time will you come
And these foes you save me from?

But even in my pain I see
Your loving hand that guideth me.
And in the still night growing dark
With empty soul and life so stark,
I know you will my pain assuage
And stay with me throughout the age.
And from before the tears I cried
And on this bed of death I lied,
You heard the words I hadn't said
And walked the steps I hadn't tread.
And for my cries there is no wrath
Because you understand my path.
Because you've walked this earth before
You know the pain it has in store.
You promise someday I'll be free
Then live with you eternally.

D. P. Myers

7

Lord, save me from the wicked man—
His words, his works, his evil plan.
Lord, let the evil that he sows
Come back to him so all may know
That you do not sit idly by
But pierce the heart with your keen eye.
You see the heart of wickedness.
You swing the sword of righteousness.
But for the hearts that righteous are
You build a refuge near and far.
In present time your help does come
And in the future save us from
Your judgment of all men on earth
And hold us in your holy mirth.

But, Lord, I wonder if it's true
These evil men that you subdue
Seem long to stand and punish all,
'Specially those whom on you call.
They dig a pit for righteous soul
But never fall they in that hole.
The righteous men they do entrap
And goodness from their souls they sap.
Their accusations false they toss
To good men's ruin—what a loss.
These evil men it seems to me
Live lives of freedom totally.
Lord, will your judgment you withhold
From evil men who live so bold?

But then I also wonder long
If I to evil do belong.
For even though to you I shout
My heart I know both in and out.
I know the evil hiding there

And oft it's more than I can bear.
And if these wicked men ought die,
O Lord, I know that so should I.
Lord, will you stay your judging hand
So knees can bow that once did stand?
They stood so strong and you defied,
But such are men for whom you died.
Lord, such was I, you know in truth,
And such are all men from their youth.

Lord, help me well to live my life
And hold to you and not to strife,
So when death's door stands open wide,
I'll walk through them with you beside.

8

Born into a fam'ly royal
Over mountain tree and soil
    Over fish and bird and beast
    From the greatest to the least.

Of all the creatures in the land,
In holy image man was planned—
    Holy each and ev'ry one
    Made in likeness of the Son.

Your glory set in heaven high
Your work is seen throughout the sky
    Yet the babe on earth below
    Is your tool to still your foe.

The babe in manger, Son of God
Yet other men you've chose—that's odd.
    Why choose men of sinful heart
    In your plan to play a part?

D. P. Myers

Will some of us with wicked soul
Be used by you to make all whole?
    Can this life of mine be used
    When with evil I am fused?

Lord, in this realm so wide and vast
From future, present, and the past,
    Broken men you've chosen long
    To sing love's majestic song.

9 (Part 1)[4]

All your hand has done through time
    And through the ages past
Cometh from the love of thine
From beginning to the last.

But wicked men seek my harm
    And seek to thwart your love
Love that comes from righteous arm
With your justice from above.

Great the power of your hand
    Brought down upon their head,
Thus, no longer in the land
Will the wicked bring us dread.

---

[4] Psalm 9 and Psalm 10 in the Book of Psalms form a single, albeit incomplete, acrostic with each verse beginning with the successive letters of the Hebrew alphabet. For these poems, 9 and 10, I have utilized the acrostic form found in the corresponding Psalm by beginning the first line in each stanza with a transliterated English version of the Hebrew letters used in each Psalm. As such, these poems are two parts of the same poem and are designated as part 1 and part 2.

A New Song

Heavy was your hand brought down
    Grinding the evil man,
Taking from them their renown
And thwarting their ev'ry plan.

When before did oppressed one
    Hopelessly hide away,
Now in freedom do they run
To your fortress in bright day.

Zeal now is in the heart
    Which cometh out in song,
Telling of the Lord's grand part
In vengeance and suff'ring long.

Choose to show your grace to me
    Zestfully, Lord, I ask.
Let my heart rejoice in thee
And sing of your hands great task.

The wicked ones you have judged
    Chastising with their snares
From the land their name you smudged
And have left them with no heirs.

You say to hell that they go,
    The ones who forget you,
But the ones who seek to know
Your glories will you renew.

Know, O Lord, that long we wait
    Your plan to reveal
And the wickedness abate
Our broken hearts to heal.

D. P. Myers

10 (Part 2)

Long, O Lord, have wicked men
    Killed the poor and needy.
Long, O Lord, have we asked when,
When will you judge the greedy?

Pouring forth from wicked tongue
    Loud curses on the poor.
Evil men waylay the young,
They're heeding your laws no more.

All day long the helpless cry
    Pleading for mercy's face.
But by evil hand they die
Never once receiving grace.

Quit your silence, Lord, my God
    And judge the wicked soul.
Long on good men have they trod
And have never paid the toll.

Run to help the fatherless,
    Quickly, to give them aid.
Stomp down the mischievous,
Help the poor souls who have prayed.

Scourge the land of evil plague.
    Rescue the innocent.
Letting not thy voice be vague,
Proclaim with holy descent

You've long heard the poor cry out,
    Sounds reaching holy throne.
Then from heaven with a shout,
Descend to protect your own.

A New Song

11

Where is the mount to which I flee
    When the wicked men run free?
And the refuge to which I go
When evil men their power show?

And have I found your fortress strong?
    For your home, do I still long?
Instead do I cry scream and shout
When righteous men the wicked rout?

In rubble of dreams broke I sit
    And cry about life's dark pit.
Since freely do the wicked roam,
There is no safe place to call home.

But promises you offer all
    On your throne stands justice tall.
Yet righteous men you often test
Before you give eternal rest.

And evil men who strike your sons,
    Putting good men on the run,
Will finally meet your righteous hand
Their souls to live in hellish lands.

Yet even so, my Lord, I pray,
    With eyes cast low now I say,
So long your testing hand I bear
So long that now I wonder where,

Where is the refuge for my soul?
    When to heal my heart's hole?
And of the promises you've told
To modern men and men of old,

D. P. Myers

How shall I trust in them just now
    When the wicked you allow
To chase the righteous man afar
And leave to wonder where you are?

O Lord, I pray the day to haste
    When your mercy I will taste.
Then songs I'll sing to you above
For eyes of mine will see your love.

Your righteous hand will guide my life
    Striking down all evil strife.
And in the daily life I live
I'll know the hope that you will give.

12

Sitting here before a mirror
I to you draw ever nearer.
For in the looking glass I see
The man who you want me to be
The man who loves your words of gold
His life in you so ever bold.
You love the lips that speak the truth
And feet that follow you from youth.
You love the hands that feed the poor
And house the needy evermore.

But oft' the face I see look back
Reveals the love that heart doth lack—
A soul that only loves the Word
And sounds of tinkling brass it's heard.
A soul that stays inside its room
And lives within a verbal tomb.
Its words have buried love so deep

That oft' your laws it doesn't keep.
It speaks of love to other men
But lives within a selfish den.

Lord, break the glass, or break the soul
That lives in such a lonely hole.
Oh, free this man from chains that bind
And keeps him living in his mind
With mental chains that bind his wrists
And tighten grip of his clenched fists.
Let the mirror show to this man
That loving others is your plan.
Your words through glass it should reveal
How every soul your love will heal.

13

When pain has plowed the soil
    And doubt is seeded deep
Then all of life is toil
    Before eternal sleep.

The fruit of doubt is hatred
    Of all that can be seen
Especially all related
    To head, heart, and between.

And oft' the wicked farmer
    Who sows the seeds of doubt
Is found to be no other
    Than he from whom they sprout.

'Tis true that other plowmen
    Can furrow deep the rows
That helps bring forth more doubt when
    It seems that God doth doze.

D. P. Myers

Then in such times of silence
    When weeds grow strong and fast,
My life hangs in the balance
    'Tween vine and weedy mast.

But if the Lord had weeded
    This heart and soul of mine,
Then doubt might not have seeded
    And light of his would shine.

Shining out from ev'ry fruit
    And from the plants so strong,
This self of mine would then root
    In love's eternal song.

And these eyes would not grow dim
    Before the wicked man
Saw my confidence in him,
    The ever-spotless Lamb.

The Lamb who never left me
    In ever-darkened times,
Even when I could not see
    That he had left some signs.

Oft' the signs of love tall stand
    When eye looks to the past
Seeing ever-loving hand
    That always held me fast.

14

Am I the fool, O Lord, my God?
Do I upon your children trod?
Do you and love my heart reject
    And only self-protect?

If you all men below doth shun
And from your righteous laws doth run,
Then I must also be a man
    Who loves a wicked plan.

But somewhere deep within my soul
I sense a longing to be whole,
I long for you to clean my heart
    And grant me a new start.

Lord, help me your protection be
To those less fortunate than me.
Lord, help my heart and soul to break
    The poor your love to take.

15

Nine of ten is not enough
    to live on holy hill.
One of ten is all it takes
    to show a sinful will.

Lord, how proud I often am
    when one of these I keep,
Yet how soon do I forget
    the sin of mine runs deep.

Is it true all other men
    struggle the way I do?
And they ever always break
    the laws that come from you?

How can men live in your tent
    if all are broken souls,
Unless someone you send to us
    will ever make us whole?

D. P. Myers

Then we'll live within your house
    on hill that's lifted high,
Having all eternity
    to you draw ever nigh.

16

The drink of gods in chalice gold
Was offered to the men of old
And offered to all men through time
And often claimed to be sublime.

But lip and teeth its stain destroys
It poisons all of Adam's boys
Neither do the girls of Eve
Find from its grip any reprieve.

It offers freedom to all men
But prisons all within its pen,
A jail of filth, disease, and death
Endured by all until last breath.

This golden chalice lifted high
Can only offer death's last sigh.
But there's another cup I know
Filled up with living water's flow.

The cup is made from humble wood
And given us by one who stood
Between God's wrath and sinful man
Fulfilling God's eternal plan.

When water from this cup I sip,
From wooden cup raised to my lip,
The stains on teeth are washed away
And poison's work this flow does stay.

A New Song

And humble though this cup might be
Its cleansing work is plain to see
The water flows to make me whole
To purge and clean my darkened soul.

A life eternal does it give,
And life abundant now I live.
Yet even though its drink is strong,
My heart, I find, does often long,

It longs for stagnant water's taste,
Old painful joys and mortal waste.
It often longs to free the sin
That dormant lies so deep within.

My darkened mind so often thinks
That if from chalice gold I drink,
Then struggles in this life will fly
And joyful life I'll not deny.

Lord, help my taste to choose a'right
And from the chalice gold take flight,
Then drink from wooden humble cup
That comes from you for me to sup.

17

O Lord, I know you save the one
Who comes to you on bended knee
Who from his wickedness will run
And rests in purity with thee.

And, Lord, I know you punish those
The wicked men who harm the poor.
You punish evil men who rose
By trampling good men evermore.

D. P. Myers

But what about this wicked man
Who pens these words to you each day?
Will me you reach with holy plan
And cleanse my life of wicked ways?

I want to say my tongue is pure
And that my feet walk righteous paths,
But evil heart I can't obscure
You see my inner clouds of wrath.

You know in me there is no good
And that my soul is painted dark,
But, Lord, you know that if I could
I'd want to be scarred by your mark.

The mark that always calls me out
From wicked men that me surround,
The mark that never leaves a doubt
That I was lost but now am found.

The mark that finds me in your arms,
Your arms that keep me from the traps
Laid down by those who seek my harm,
Not knowing that your arms will wrap—

They wrap me close to you in time.
They clear the path I walk upon.
They show to all that I am thine
For now and in eternal dawn.

18

Do I treat you as my rock?
Is your word in my heart locked?
Do I seek you through the day?
Do I let you guide my way?

    In times of trouble do I fly
        and seek you, Lord, who sit on high?
    Or do I lonely venture out
        and in my trouble cry and pout?

Have I had a life that's pure?
Can I stand before you sure?
Do I come on humble knee?
Or is pride so plain to see?

    When foes around me stand so tall,
        are you the one to whom I call?
    And when my enemies close in,
        do you I trust or do I sin?

Even David with his flaws
Was your servant for just cause.
So I hope you me employ,
Letting not my sin destroy.

19

Deep down within my soul there lies
    A nature full of darkened sin,
Yet naught is hidden from your eyes
    Your holy eyes pierce deep within.

D. P. Myers

And from within me there flows out
    My words and actions that betray
The inner man without a doubt
    Through everything I do and say.

The mediations of my heart
    And words that fall from off my tongue
I hope that both of these take part
    In wisdom and the truth you've sung.

You've sung your love in deepest space
    That only silent heart can know,
Then holy words you gave our race
    Your inner thoughts through them you show.

The holy words to man you gave
    Should help the words I speak be true
And in my heart should also pave
    A road of thought that pleases you.

20

Do I call you when in trouble,
    or do I just complain?
Do I call when life's in rubble,
    or do I trust your reign?

Some will place their trust in horses
    and some their trust in gold,
Some will never trust in sources
    that come from you of old.

But you ever always listen
    when I cry out your name,
And from heaven me you christen
    with your love o'er my shame.

Yet the love you freely give me
    often seems so absent,
When your help I can't foresee
    my hopeful heart is rent.

Lord, open blind eyes to perceive
    Your love that still abides,
And make me willing to receive
    Your helpful hand that guides.

Then when darkened times of testing
    break and crash on life's shore,
Teach me always to be trusting
    Your love forevermore.

21

Lord, help me trust in the work you have done
That has not yet been seen under the sun.
    For the righteous are already yours,
    On the wicked your wrath ever pours.
So help me trust in the war you have won.

You promise long life to all who believe,
Yet often in life there is no reprieve
    From the wicked men's stark insolence
    And their evil and dark violence.
Help me to trust even though I oft' grieve.

The strength that you give is cause for great song,
Yet I am so weak and oft' suffer long
    Under evil men's sinister lies,
    Which are spoken in front of your eyes.
Remember, O Lord, to you I belong.

D. P. Myers

Lord, help me to walk with strength through each day
And trust in your love along life's rough way,
    So even when wicked men rail
    And times when I stumble and fail,
Meet me with love so on your path I'll stay.

22

Life's bulls and lions come in forms
    So diff'rent for all men,
But blows and teeth that cut us all
    Come time and time again.

There seems to be no respite from
    The tangling whips of foes,
They rip the heart and tie the feet
    Wherever we all go.

Our hearts are like a pool so deep
    That time has calmed and stilled,
But often words from foe or friend
    This placid life have killed.

From deep abyss their words dredge up
    The knowledge we are worm.
These rocky words tossed in life's pond
    The worm in me confirms.

But I've been told the God on high
    Has chosen me from birth,
And in the womb his hand has formed
    A son of his on earth.

A New Song

But if I'm truly God's dear one
    Down here in dusty land,
Then why does trouble haunt me so
    And sneak past holy hand?

I thought his hand was meant to keep
    Me safe from evil's harm,
Instead at night it often seems
    I'm held in wicked arms.

And morn's bright light through glassy panes
    My eyes they often greet
With weakened heart from last dark night
    That bare' can move my feet.

I often wish that men before
    Had spoken with clear words
About your work within their life,
    Your good words that they'd heard.

But muted tongue is no excuse
    For how my life has flowed,
For in the end I only, Lord,
    I only bear that load.

Lord, help me now to seek for you
    Through pleasure and in pain,
And know the love you always give
    Through each for me is gain.

And also, Lord, free my mute tongue
    To ever sing your praise
To those I know and those to come
    A help through darkened days.

23

Lord, you know that deep within
    I want for many things,
        But cold the icy hand of sin
        That turns my fleshy heart to tin
        So that to you I do not bring
        The wants that lay so deep therein.

How, O Lord, can I now live
    Through ev'ry darkened night,
        Unless to me some help you give
        So every sin I won't relive
        Through all my life's long troubled plight
        For such your blood from cross forgives.

Still I know you walk with me
    Along life's troubled way,
        And it's in you that I am free
        From sinful troubles that I see.
        My darkened night is now the day
        And restful life's now found with thee.

Such a love from you does show
    Along with me you walk,
        And with me here on earth below
        Through all my troubles now I know
        That I am part of holy flock
        And guided by love's staff I go.

A New Song

24

Often, Lord, my soul it bends
    my heart befriends
    and hand extends
        to what is false.

Also, Lord, I seek your face
    desire grace
    and your embrace
        for it is right.

Help me in this constant war
    to sin abhor
    and you adore
        for you are good.

Open wide this heart of mine
    so in will shine
    your love divine
        and make me pure.

May I live on holy hill
    and can you fill
    me with your will
        so I am yours.

Then, Lord, at the end of life
    beyond all strife
    with goodness rife
        please take me home.

D. P. Myers

25

How grand it is, my Lord and God,
    That sinners such as I
Can bow the knee and humbly nod
    And from me shame will fly.

For all the sins I know I've done
    An ever-blackened mark,
And all my days under the sun
    I've filled with evil dark.

And there are sins that I know not
    I've done with blinded eyes,
My soul such sins doth wholly rot
    The goodness in me dies.

But to this soul so full of sin
    Much evil looks so fine,
And wicked men's dark traps begin
    To look like freedom's sign.

Yet deeper still your word does rest
    In souls that you do choose,
So in the end we'll pass the test
    Our foes hope that we lose.

The humble knee that bows to you
    Bows only by your grace,
And by your words you make us new
    So we can see your face.

Bright from your face pure love does shine
    Into this troubled soul,
Renewing in me your design
    To ever make me whole.

26

I am walking with the Lord
    Along life's wand'ring way.
Level pathways leading toward
    The house where he does stay.

Moving always toward his love
    In faith each step I take.
Guidance coming from above
    I, sinful ways, forsake.

But this path is often strewn
    With rocks I stumble on;
Rocks that evil men have hewn,
    Rocks now they sit upon.

Sitting now they call to me;
    They tell me now to rest.
All their words say that I'll see,
    I'll see their way is best:

"There's no house found down this path,
    This path you walk along.
There is no God bringing wrath
    To those who sing our song.

Sit and rest your weary feet
    And sing with us this verse,
Telling others that we meet
    That walking is a curse."

There are times these words of theirs
    Have drawn my eyes from you,
And their life without a care
    Seems vibrant and so true.

D. P. Myers

But I think back on the good
    That came from holy hands.
Then I know I never could
    Forget your promised lands:

Lands that lay at path's far end
    Where holy hill is found,
Hill that one day I'll ascend
    And by you there be crowned—

Crowned for lifting up my eyes
    And walking down life's road
Knowing that my self must die
    To live in your abode.

Keep me walking with you, Lord,
    Along life's wand'ring way.
Level pathways lead me toward
    The house where we will stay.

27

Foes surround and taunt me
    Seeking my demise
Saying not to trust thee,
Will you avert your eyes?

False the accusations
    Rooted in lie's dirt
Seeking life's cessation,
Will you allow the hurt?

True, my nature's fallen,
    Yes, I've done much wrong,
But these lies they're telling,
Will you endure their song?

A New Song

I often hide away
    From these foes of mine.
I have become their prey,
Will you protect, Lord, thine?

In my heart's deep crying,
    Lord, I seek your face.
For your home I'm longing,
Will you prepare a place?

Will you show your beauty?
    Will your face you show?
Will you love love's duty,
So you in life I'll know?

28

How do I know that when I cry
    The rock on high has ears?
From birth until the day I die
    My life is full of tears.

How do I know that evil men
    Will face their just reward?
The evil men seem to have been
    In wickedness ignored.

The promises that came from you,
    They tell me not to fret,
For all the souls that you renew
    You never will forget.

And all those men with evil hearts
    You someday will destroy,
Then banish to the hellish parts
    Away from heaven's joy.

D. P. Myers

Lord, hear the cry that lies within
    Each person's darkened soul,
For though it's true that all men sin,
    Lord, won't you make them whole?

I often seem like those you hate,
    The ones you promise death,
But you have opened heaven's gate
    For me by Spirit's breath.

You've built a refuge high above
    This earthly battleground
And paved the entrance with your love
    For me whom you have found.

You heard my cry; your strength you gave
    To me when I was low,
So then when I'm beyond the grave
    To holy rock I'll go.

29

Weak the cries that rise to you
    Up from this life of pain.
Stronger are the voices from
    The angels who help reign.

But no voice in all the realms
    Compare to holy tongue,
Giving life to all that is
    When forming note was sung.

Clear and strong your voice rang out
    You brought all things to life
Menacing and damning too,
    Your voice will end all strife.

A New Song

Powerful and bold your voice,
    It's like none else I know,
But it rings with mercy too
    For sinners here below.

Who can stand before the Lord
    When voice of his rings out?
Only foolish ones with pride
    Who raise their fist and shout.

"Freedom now we want from you,
    We want to go our way
Evermore to live apart
    From all that you will say.

Furthermore, we hate the fact
    That only you create.
Give us time, and you will see
    The powers we will make"

Foolish are the ones who yell
    Such hatred at your throne,
For the powers that they have
    They come from you alone.

Even voices that they use
    Are given by your hand,
All they have you can remove
    From them by your command.

Help me, Lord, to use my voice
    In all humility,
Singing praise to you on high
    For all the earth to see.

D. P. Myers

Let them see your mighty work
    And all the love you give,
Saving fallen from their sin
    And making dead men live.

30

So steep the path before
    That winds through caverns grim,
Not knowing what's in store
    In light ahead so dim.

The pathways I have tread
    Through darkest caves so deep,
They never once have led
    To treasures I can keep.

The baubles that are found
    In pits so far below,
By them all men are bound,
    His face to never know.

But you are not so dense
    To not have heard my cry,
You call me far from whence
    If I would stay I'd die.

You lift me from the pit,
    Bringing me close to you,
And all my sins acquit
    As you have made me new.

You take me from my sin
    And build for me a place
Where I can walk within
    And clearly see your face.

A New Song

31

Hand so righteous of the Lord,
    Ubiquitous it is.
Troubled pathways I can ford
    Held firm by hand of his.

Up he lifts from troubled fray
    From dangers all around,
Keeping me until the day
    When holy trumpets sound.

Paths are cleared and rocks removed,
    The ground is ever strong.
Straight the road that he approved
    For me my whole life long.

Even with a path so straight
    Laid out before my feet,
Wicked men and traps await,
    Both in this life I'll meet.

Hands of evil men reach out,
    My feet they hope to trip.
When I stumble, then I doubt
    His promised holy grip.

In that moment on the dirt
    With tears upon my face,
In that moment full of hurt
    I long for His embrace.

Slow at times his hand will come,
    Then I quick turn to sin.
In my weakness I succumb
    To dark desires within.

D. P. Myers

Cold the hands of wicked men
    That touch my fallen form,
Pulling me to darkened den,
    They say my sin's the norm.

While away I'm being pulled
    There comes another tug,
Your warm hands that want to hold
    Me in a loving hug.

Strong your grip that holds me tight,
    My doubts they soon depart.
Your strong hands begin to fight
    For me and for my heart.

When each battle has been won
    You place my hand in yours.
Like anew my life's begun,
    My heart within me soars.

All through life your mighty hand
    Is always holding me,
But I think I lonely stand,
    Clear eyes I need to see.

Let me see the work you do
    And know that you are there,
Or in blindness trust in you
    And rest long in your care.

32

Two men have I at times been through my life:
One silent, keeping secret sins inside.
Troubled days, walking pathways long in strife,

A New Song

Swimming against the ever-swelling tide.
Wishing often a sympathetic ear,
And loving friends to hold me close and cry.
But in those times when friends have drawn so near,
My lips are closed, my eyes avert, I fly.
In loneliness and shame I walk so long,
By barbs and whips I ever know my way.
Mournful voice singing always its one song,
I numbly tread through every darkened day.
These empty steps familiar to me still,
If walked for long, my soul they'd rape and kill.

But second man of late have I become,
Naked standing, exposed before the Lord.
To piercing eyes of his will I succumb,
And by his hands my guilty streams I'll ford.
On other side so far away from guilt,
The paths I'll walk are ever in his care.
In stormy days a safe place has he built
To keep my soul from walking in despair.
Instead of whips his staff directs me now,
Teaching ever the way I ought to live.
And on those days when troubled is my brow,
Forgiveness, love, and more he has to give.
As the second man, nothing do I lack.
To the first, I hope I never will go back.

33

My strength I can't rely upon
    To get me through each day,
But all the battles you have won
    They pave for me a way.

D. P. Myers

Never is life's path so easy,
    In fact, at times it's hard.
Though it often does not please me
    It, sinful ways retard.

Life's rocky pathways lead me toward
    The place where I should be,
A place where I am with you, Lord,
    And you, through life, with me.

Long through these troubled days we go
    On earth formed by your word.
An earth that by its beauties show
    Your glories never heard.

These glories from you to me bring
    A heart so glad and strong,
And then from lips of mine I sing
    A new and holy song.

A song of praise, a battle cry
    From you my lips will sound,
As enemies before us fly
    When tread we life's tough ground.

34

Driven from the work he gave.
    Accused by evil men.
Crying out to he who saves,
    Defend my life again.
Keep me from the tongues that lie
    And those that seek my life.
Guard my days with watchful eye,
    Lord, keep me from harm's strife.

A New Song

In your strength will then I rest
    Your justice I'll adore,
Under mercy's wing I'm blessed
    And loved forevermore,
        I'm loved forevermore.

Yet these paths anew I tread
    Are never free from pain.
Doubts and pressures I still dread
    Come quick to me again.
Troubles old and troubles new
    I often will attract.
Troubles then I give to you
    When I'm under attack.
Your pure love it comforts me
    When in this darkened plight.
And clear exits then I see
    By your amazing light,
        In your amazing light.

35

"How long, O Lord," my cry persists,
    "Must I wait for justice' hand?"
The righteous under evil fists
    For long I cannot stand.

The lies they tell about your son
    Evermore upon their lips.
The battle seeming to be won,
    My life within their grip.

My silent tongue it longs to sing
    Clear and loud out to your throne,
"Lord, when will you your judgment bring
    To safe keep all your own?"

D. P. Myers

But long do sins of mine they haunt
    All along life's winding way,
And wicked men from past they taunt,
    "Unchanged," is what they say.

Repentant is my weeping heart,
    Always longing for your touch,
Your breath of life, a fresh new start,
    I need these, Lord, so much.

But till such time I'm free from strife,
    Keep my feet from paths of sin.
So at the end of troubled life
    I'll through your gates walk in.

36

For many days and many nights
I saw my life by my own light.
My light to darkness on my bed,
When evil thoughts woke in my head—
They filled my heart and bent my ways,
Your light cast out by my dark days.
But blame on you I cannot cast
Right judgment should be on me vast.
But out from you instead comes love
Poured down from heavens high above.
Righteous and faithful have you been
Your steadfast love to me again.
There is no worth found in my life
That you should free me from my strife.
But love flows from your nature pure,
The promises from you are sure,
And from your fountain also flows
Your light and life, so you I know.

A New Song

And now upon my bed I see
Anew by light that comes from thee.

37

My heart is wrung by evil's stand.
It's taken over your good land.
It's mocked and sneered your righteous hand.

> You have told me not to fret
> Judgment will you not forget,
> On the evil vile set.
> They for righteous are a threat,
> Ever will they pay their debt,
> Cast away then to forget.
>
> Yet prosper now these evil men.
> They seem to triumph. Lord, what then?
> Will goodness come to me again?
> Lord, oft' I wonder *When, O when?*
>
> Even so I seek your light,
> Ways of yours are always right.

But someday they you'll cast away,
And ever in your land I'll stay
In righteous fortress every day.

38

Days have come, and days have gone,
Burdens have I carried long.
Sins of mine loom in the past,
Shadow o'er this day is cast.

D. P. Myers

Sin still tempts me in the night,
It still tempts me in the light.
Where my feet have found to tread,
Burden follows, bringing dread.
From the past, old voices haunt,
Making face and body gaunt.
Yes, I know that you forgive,
And new life to me you give.
Yes, to you my mute voice cries,
But my ears still hear their lies.
Lord, I'm waiting to be free
From the lying chains on me.
Though you've paid my sin's full debt,
Foolish past I can't forget.
Voices false far from me take,
Purge me from regretful ache.
Life so true I long to know,
Free from chains I want to grow.
Till the time that I'm not bound,
Lord, let my hope in you be found.

39

Lord, you give and then you take,
What of this life shall I make?

Shall I spend my days in tears
Hiding from my darkest fears?

Or to walk with you so bold
All my days from young to old?

Will you let me cry and shout
Asking what this life's about?
Do you want my tongue to cease,
Troubled days alone in peace?

A New Song

Life so short, is that your plan?
Not just me, but every man—
Shadows, dust, a phantom's life,
Days of good and days of strife.

How, Lord, can I seek and find
Pleasures on this life's long grind?
Or are pleasures only found
After you our life have ground?

Do you want me on my knees,
Folded hands, will you that please?
Do you want my head bowed low,
Humble life for me to know?

Lord, I know my life is short,
Ending days will soon report.
Help me know the way to live
That to you will pleasure give.

Lord, you give, and then you take,
Most of this life help me make.

40

A song of self I used to sing
But solace this song did not bring.
    Song of lust and bawdy deeds,
    Satisfying selfish needs,
    Such song sung had planted weeds.

Then one day in weedy garden
Seeking from old song a pardon,
    I heard song that sounded new.
    Longing deep within me grew,
    To leave false song for the true.

D. P. Myers

It came to me in darkest night
Igniting in my heart a light.
    To me drawing oh so near,
    Voice so pure and ever clear,
    Broke my heart and drew a tear.

The steady light then grew so strong
And in the night came this new song,
    Clearing out my darkened heart,
    Taking selfish soul apart,
    Giving to me a new start.

And from this song anew I found
A cultivated sacred ground,
    Strength to pull the weed's tough shoot
    From the leaf down to the root,
    Crushing plant under my boot.

Then springing forth from sacred plot
And by this new song I've been taught,
    Myrtle vines that far do sprawl,
    Flowers, plants, and trees so tall,
    Holy fruit comes from them all.

But even with this land so plush
At times from me will old song gush,
    Sacred ground old song will heave
    Killing plants and burning leaves,
    Causing broken heart to grieve.

I need your help to not forget
The song in me you did beget.
    Help me sing it every day.
    Give me all the words to say.
    Let your new song guide my way.

41

Bountiful table for me you have set
Delectable bread from your hand to mine.
Much more from your hand can I always get
You're constantly giving all that is thine.
Even with heaven's bread that is so good
There's oft' an ill voice that stirs in my heart.
With gratitude gone it says that I should
Decry the goodness you've giv'n on my part.
Your beauty before me captures my sight,
Yet something within me longs far to run,
To seek other pleasures in darkest night
Instead of sweet mercies found in your Son.
Lord, light this dark heart that evil's long led.
Let me dine solely on your living bread.

Responses to Book Two of the Psalms: 42 – 72

42

Links I've added one by one
    Drag down my lonely heart.
Into shadow from the sun
    I from my joy did part.

Lips of mine once sang so free
    New songs for all to hear.
Choices took me far from thee
    Where darkness gathers near.

D. P. Myers

Links were forged each step I took
    And long have grown my chains,
Weighing down this soul that looks
    At all my self-made pains.

Eyes cast low yet long to rise
    And see your holy face.
But the chains I now despise
    Keep me from seeing grace.

In the dark I know it's true
    That I have forged each link.
Even so I long for you
    While weighted soul doth sink.

Let your painful hammer fall
    And cut each link away.
Freely then my voice will call
    To you in dawning day.

43

Far away in desert dry
    Where night consumes time's hands,
My soul weeps and loudly cries:
    I long to leave dead lands.

Spinning hands have brought no light
    To show my feet the way.
Circl'ling in the gloomy night,
    Where is the dawn of day?

Voices from the shadows call
    My head drops down in shame.
My past sins they speak of all
    The ways you I defame.

A New Song

Have you gone, do you reject,
    Are you for me no more?
Will you not again protect
    And love me evermore?

Please silence all the voices,
    Each one that cries, "Despair!"
Then help me make good choices
    And sinful paths forswear.

Send your guiding light to me
    And lead me from this place.
Take me from the dark to see
    Your holy loving face.

44

Years ago I've heard it told
Works of yours from days of old—
Doors were opened by your hand
Leading to a promised land,
Walls that fell before your gaze,
Pris'ners freed from darkened days—
All your works so clear to see
Ne'er to doubt the loving three.

But if words I honest speak
Hope and joy are growing weak.
Daily though I read your Word
When was last your voice I heard?
Prayers still I offer high
But my blinded eyes still cry,
"Are you in my life just now?
Help me see, I know not how."

D. P. Myers

Why do I in gloomy state
On your Word now so long wait?
Is it that I know you love
Even with dark clouds above?
Or when doors are locked so tight
Through the cracks I see your light?
Is it that I know you're true
That I wait so long on you?

Keep me pure in times of doubt.
Keep me till the trump sounds out.
Keep me walking in your way.
Light my path until you say,
"You've done well, my patient son.
Lonely path I've had you run.
Enter now. Please walk inside.
Rest in love's eternal tide."

45

Along all time across the earth
The only way to find our worth
The only cause you see as good
When righteous men for truth have stood.
Your blessings may be opulent
Some gold for love and marriage spent
And sons you give to carry on
A name to those of future dawn.
But no gift comes from you above
Unless your righteousness I love
Unless I fight for cause of truth
To dying day and from my youth.

Lord, make me wait before your throne
Till holy love becomes my own.
Guide sure the steps I take each day

Throughout my life until you say,
"Now come to me my holy bride
And live forever at my side.
Now sit beside eternal throne
Endless joy to be your own.
Forever love to you I give
And evermore with me you'll live."
Until that day please make of me
A righteous vessel kept for thee.

46

The temp'ral fabric of my life
    Is nevermore the same.
Past happy times, now days of strife,
    No solid stitch remains.

The ground, it shakes beneath my feet,
    The trees, they tumble down.
The earth, it burns with fervent heat,
    All covered by death's gown.

But I've been told there is a place,
    A rock to stand upon,
A place to ever go for grace
    And see the new day's dawn.

A fortress built in heaven high
    That never shall be moved,
It reaches down from holy sky
    Its strength is ever proved.

This place, this fortress of the Lord
    Keeps me in troubled times,
Through days when on my life is poured
    A punishment for crimes.

D. P. Myers

My guilt will someday pass away.
    My life will he renew.
In stillness then I'll hear him say,
    "I always did love you."

47

What flaw resides under my skin
That keeps all songs locked deep within?
From where has come this inner chain
That holds my heart in constant pain?
Why to you can I not sing praise
And voice of joy high to you raise?

O Lord, you've gone out with a shout.
All enemies of mine you rout.
You walk me down a pleasant path.
You keep me from eternal wrath.
You've given me a fam'ly fair.
So why, oh why, do I despair?

I want to sing out praise to you.
I want a voice that's loud and true.
I want to sing of how you're near.
I want a voice that rings so clear.
Some joy to you I wish to bring
With voice that all your praises sing.

Forgive this darkened lowly soul
With broken heart that is not whole.
Forgive this voice that has gone mute
Like king to beast, a prideful brute.
Forgive this one with senses dull
Whose ears can't hear your trump's clear call.

A New Song

Lord, break the chains that bind my heart
Release me now to sing my part.
Let voice of mine join heaven's throng
As to you we lift joyful song.
Now free me, Lord, to use my voice
So here on earth I will rejoice.

48

I've been told of fortress strong
    tall towers to the sky.
It's been sung in ancient song
    before it men will fly.

Enemies have pressed the walls
    foundation rock runs deep.
Soon in battle foes all fall
    before this massive keep.

Stately gates atop the hill
    sole entrance to be found.
'fore it men of iron will
    fall humbly to the ground.

Only can the humble walk
    through gates that bar their way.
Through these gates of living rock
    they hear the keeper say,

"Enter in, my faithful son,
    this city by my grace.
By the battles I have won
    when I built you this place."

D. P. Myers

Open wide the gates will swing
    and humble man will stand.
In the distance voices sing,
    "Come in to city grand!"

Walking in on dusty feet
    onto the streets of gold.
There the keeper will he meet,
    "I'll wash your feet," he's told.

After cleansing tender touch
    he's led through city vast.
Finding riches there with such
    deep beauty that will last.

Years and years will not provide
    time for the wealth that's here.
Time to know all gems inside
    within the city's tiers.

Many years have passed since I
    walked through those humble gates.
Soon will come my day to die,
    true city now awaits.

But in days that I am old,
    so distant from my youth.
I'll seek the ones to be told
    of beauty's richest truth.

Then one day in holy realm
    all ages far and wide
Will stand 'fore eternal helm,
    scarred keeper at our side.

A New Song

49

Why, O Lord, do I fear
    The words and ways of man?
Why can men bring a tear?
    Depressed I often am.

Darkened clouds on my brow,
    A paralyzing storm.
Shuffling feet, shoulders bow,
    Such weight does me deform.

When will eye see your light
    A'breaking through the clouds?
Will this storm soon take flight
    Removing gloomy shrouds?

Men, I know, hold no threat
    To my eternal soul.
You alone pay the debt
    That keeps me from Sheol.

Let me not soon forget
    The love you have for me.
Let their words not beset
    Me as I wait for thee.

50

"Duty," calls the holy man,
"Sacrifice is God's sole plan.
Stoic must I walk each day
If to God I'll find my way.
Daily toil pleases him,
Trudging plow, a life so grim.

D. P. Myers

Head cast down with dragging feet
Hope that works my sins defeat."

Ground of works begins to shake.
Looking 'round the full earth quakes.
Lifting up my lowly eye,
Beauty's form in fortress high.
Judgment's fire him before
Clouds and tempest near him soar.
Voice like mighty sea calls out
Clear his words like trumpet shout,

"Stop your grudging sacrifice
All your work will ne'er suffice.
Do you think I need a thing
That to me you sadly bring?
Joy I've wanted in your life
From your lips thanksgiving rife.
And your ways on paths so pure
With my truth that guides you sure."

When I looked in beauty's face
Over me poured out his grace.
Nothing that I'd ever done
Had salvation from him won.
Only did he want from me
Thanks for all and purity.
His salvation is a gift
Only he can bridge the rift.

Someday close to him I'll walk.
Intimately will we talk.
He will tell me of his love
And his Father high above.
But before that day I know
Through the fire I must go.
Burning dross from broken soul
By his fire I'm made whole.

A New Song

51

How quickly, Lord, I move
Into my comfort's groove.
How quickly am I blind
No mystery do I find.
Your word becomes so dull
I cannot see at all.

I look at pages thin
And know there's depth within.
But all that I can see
Is what I've made of thee.
An idol of my thoughts
A finite god I've wrought.

My sin, I used to think,
Was only when I'd drink
Of fleshly passion's cup
Drunk down with lusty sup
Drunk deep with vice and greed
Fulfilling selfish need.

But now the sin I know
So subtle does it grow
Into a love of facts
And to familiar acts
Then sacrifices dull
That you don't love at all.

Create in me a new
Fresh heart that can love you,
Two hands that ne'er will build
Mute idols that are filled
With mem'ries of the past
Forms dead that cannot last.

D. P. Myers

Please let me live again
Away with all my sin,
And open these blind eyes
To see the truth from lies,
And make my heart contrite
To sacrifice aright
And ever live in light.

52

What great trouble is the tongue—
    Lying words it has sung.
    An evil song begun.

Is it greater than the man
    Who plots an evil plan?
    Works wicked then began.

Words or works, which one is worse:
    Darkened deeds, darkened verse?
    Each from a sinful curse.

Both I think these must be wrong:
    Bloody hands, broken song.
    Each still I suffer long.

Both make marks on my weak soul
    'larging heart's blackened hole,
    Broken man not yet whole.

Oh, that I could trust in thee,
    Not lies coming from me
    But your blood setting me free.

53

The words of lips may often part
From uttered phrases of the heart.
The speech that rolls off silky tongue
Oft' won't compare to heart's verse sung,
For deep within the honest soul
Is living rock and empty hole.

From empty hole comes speech and hand
Denying he who rules the land,
Denying he who sits above,
Denying Son who died in love,
And all its works and words so fine
Won't save this godless heart of mine.

But also in my heart I hold
The living rock from which I'm told
Redeem my words and works it will,
Redeem my heart and even still,
Redeem my life from terror's cry,
And then no shame for when I die.

O, that my verse won't make of me
A fool for all around to see.
Lord, keep my tongue and mold my way
So that my words and heart will say,
"There is a God above us all
Who every knee before will fall.
Now let my heart hear holy call
To enter his eternal hall."

54

Patience, Lord, I want to have
    In the face of trials long.
Spread your name that is a salve
    Cover all my painful wrongs.

Hurt is borne beneath my skin
    From the enemies without.
They who praise no God within,
    They continue evil rout.

Give me strength under their blows,
    Strength to not reject your name.
You in ages past arose
    Rose to cover all my shame.

Still I sit in darkest night
    In my isolation's pain,
Waiting when for me you'll fight
    So I'll see the dawn again.

Till such time with banner high
    And my foes are swept away,
Thanks to you, not painful sighs,
    Lord, please help my heart to say.

55

How simple my life seems to be
When in plain sight the enemy
Before me stands as evil man
Working out his wicked plan.

A New Song

When I raise my sword and shield
Fight ensues, and soon he yields,
Then to his knees my foe falls down,
"The Lord's strength!" a cry renown.

But not all foes will show their face
Some lurk and slink in darkened place,
Some walk beside me hand in hand,
Others live in inward land.

The foes of mine that creep about
Stab in the dark. Then I cry out.
I cry to him who sits on high.
Justice from him then will fly.

And of the foes once I called friend,
Faces shimmer at desert's end.
Love's oasis in soul's dark wells.
Mouth of sand my parched soul fells.

But still the cuts that hurt the most
Come not from distant fleshy host.
Deadly foe resides much nearer,
Face that's seen in the mirror.

My words and works of distant past
Builds scar on scar that long will last.
This flesh deformed is silent not,
Words accuse to my soul's rot.

All of these foes in time will find
The hidden scars that slay my mind.
Their piercing swords scar flesh below,
Tender pain to searing grows.

D. P. Myers

There was a time when I stood tall,
I battled foes external all.
But in these wars that I now wage
I fall down and can't engage.

Yet when these foes seek me to kill,
I hear a voice so small and still.
The soothing voice calls me to trust
In the Lord; to trust I must.

But him to trust I know not how
When under heavy blows I bow.
Yet turning weary head I see
His scarred palms there next to me.

And on his head a thorny crown,
A crimson trickle flowing down.
"I bear these blows so someday soon
With the Father we'll commune.

For I was sent to be with you
So battles like these you'll get through.
Now take my hand and then endure.
These wars end. My vict'rys sure."

I know he's always at my side.
In him my pains I can confide.
And though they're times I see him not,
Crimson flow has freedom bought.

I know I'm weak, but you are strong,
So help me through these battles long.
And help me through my soul's dark night
As you for me my battles fight.

56

When 'neath my feet the strong ground quakes
And starry host above me shakes,
When dark clouds turn the day to night
All barring me from living light,
From corners dark then scurries those
Whose lies the darkness won't expose.
The lies they speak are formed so well
That truth from falsehood none can tell,
And thus like goat outside the camp,
Long doomed am I to ever tramp
Down valleys low and mountains high,
I, far from man, to you draw nigh.
I come from valley of dark death
Enlivened by your holy breath,
Spurred on to lands I do not know
I follow you where're you go.
I trust in you on lighted path
That leads away from false foe's wrath.
Yet even so deep down inside
Lies heavy heart and broken pride,
It's true my pride you need to break
And of me humble man to make.
But with my heavy heart I find
That fear has taken o'er my mind,
And trusting you is hard to do,
Will you my dead heart, Lord, renew?
The heaviness within my soul
Please lift its weight; please make me whole,
For I know that the dark nights end
Then on my path your light you'll send,
And on life's ways that are not known
Might self I find; I am your own.
Do with me as you desire,
Draw me to you ever higher,
Lord, draw me in the ways you must
So in you I will learn to trust.

D. P. Myers

57

Hidden caves with foes afar
Searching, God, for where you are.
Refuge for the man within
Refuge from the men of sin.
Battles rage at darkened gate
Foes, they want to set my fate.
My voice calls in times like these,
"Come protect me, O God, please."

But where can I go to hide
From the foe that lives inside,
Corrupting heart, soul, and mind
With the evil he can find?
There's no cave for me to go
Hiding from this one I know,
From the evil one I see
Staring from the glass at me.

The grace of heaven, I've been told
Outstrips my sin eternal fold,
And through the cross of steadfast love
Pours crimson stream from God above
To cleanse the foe within my soul
And once again to make me whole
So when this ends, this life of mine,
No foes I'll find in arms of thine.

A New Song

58

I know the wicked man
Devises every plan
From deep within his heart
To from you then depart.
His steps and ways are dark,
Ne'er to correction hark,
Ne'er does he love the good
But sups on wicked food.
Yet such a man awaits
Eternally dark fate
Come from the hand of God,
By holy feet he's trod.

But should my heart rejoice
When silence you their voice?
Should face break out in grin
When they are judged for sin?
I know oppression ends
When judgment you will send,
Then righteous men are free
To seek and follow thee.
But even so, my Lord,
Please will you stay your sword
And help the wicked men
To seek your heart again?

For in the glass I spy
A dark and vile eye
That seeks not beauty's face
But ways to thwart your grace.
From bent desire's root
Comes putrid rotten fruit.
Yet out from eye's dark pools
Trickles the tears of fools,
A fool who knows his life

D. P. Myers

Is filled with evil strife
And wants so much to change,
Like me—is that so strange?

Lord, each of your dark foes
Like me they once did grow
From innocent, sweet boys
Who climbed and played with toys.
They searched and then explored,
Found ways that you deplored,
And from that fruit did taste
A juice of inner waste.
But is it deadly sure
That you cannot still cure
Their deadly dark disease
And bring them to their knees?

For nothing more than hope,
Please stay the hangman's rope.
Hope that a future day
Will see them find their way
Back to a child's state
When on you they will wait
And to your arms they'll run
And called by you a son,
Then bitter fool's tears turn
From regret's stinging burn
Into a joyful flow
In steadfast love's sweet glow.

59

From the past a voice rings clear,
Out from shadows dark deeds peer.
Mem'ries of the man I was,
Yet I'm free from this because

Years before my day of birth
You declared me of great worth,
Debts you paid upon a tree
Steadfast love you showed to me.

Still the voices cry out loud
Casting over me a shroud.
Their words spices for my death
Waiting for my dying breath.

Even though their voices ring
With a tune I once did sing,
Not all songs of theirs are true,
Shadows gone; you me renew.

Voice of mine will sing a song,
"Now to you do I belong.
Deeds and darkened ways are past,
Though I trip, your love's steadfast."

Yet for me stands a pyre
Built by lies of desire.
Rumors false of deeds I've done
And of paths I've never run.

Voices are not just without
Often self sounds evil shout,
Taunting torture in my head
Sparks the deathly wooden bed.

D. P. Myers

Devil's mask upon my soul,
Dark facade in flaming roll.
Even I am taken in
By false claims about my sin.

Voices, voices ever clear
Lapping 'round me ev'ry year.
Din of voices from all foes
Corner me in cold repose.

Frozen in a fearful state
For last breath do I now wait.
Yet I know for me you died
On the tree for me you cried.

Tears of love flow mingled down
With the blood from thorny crown.
Down the wood and to the earth,
From the fire, my rebirth.

Help this darkened soul of mine
To be lit by love of thine.
Still the voices of despair.
Fill my mouth with holy air.

Let my lips sing words of love
Of your strength from high above,
The strong fortress that you build
Promises of yours fulfilled.

Turn my black heart into white,
Vict'rys prize in holy fight
Lets my song of love ring high
Far above despairing cry.

A New Song

One last thing, Lord, do I ask—
Strength to finish my life's task
Free from lies and all false shame,
Ever you my voice proclaim.

60

Please save me, Lord, from low disgrace
    And lift a banner high
So in that place I'll see your face
    Where fearful men can fly.

But in this state, my broken state,
    I feel left alone.
I wonder if me you do hate,
    Like Saul, me you disown.

Repent I've done so many times
    Yet to my vomit go.
I oft' repeat my many crimes
    And need fresh crimson flow.

Lord, will you let me come to you
    This sad and broken man,
This man who sins each day anew
    For such is who I am?

And will my many foes you strike
    And clear the battle land—
Both in and outward foe alike—
    Then hold me in your hand?

D. P. Myers

61

I know, my God, you are above
Always watching with steadfast love.
But in this life I've traveled far
Never quite knowing where you are.

Yet even so I cry to thee
With hope that one day I will see
'Cross battle plains and standing high
Your tower strong against the sky.

Against all hope I must admit
I often thought I'd not see it.
Yet still I know my heart will leap
When seeing tower of your keep.

So lead me now to tower's base
Through battles dark to lighted place,
Through mundane fights of normal day,
And guide my feet on holy way.

Lord, guide me to this house of yours
To comfort's place where love assures,
Where love caresses by your hand
That's been with me throughout life's land.

And even though the tower's sight
Is not present, please help me fight,
Please give me strength against the foes
Who in my heart dark evil sows.

And build around my heart a wall,
A rampart that will never fall,
A fortress keeping evil out
But lets love through with joyous shout.

A New Song

Your love that kneads and keeps my heart,
Creating daily a fresh start,
A heart that's new and sings your praise
Through battles now to end of days.

Then when for me the last day dawns
And golden sun turns azure bronze,
Let my sight in final hour
See the gates of holy tower.

62

Often, Lord, I've said to you
To others and myself, 'tis true
Only rest I in your power
Every day and every hour.

Often, Lord, I bend my knee
And offer up my all to thee,
I say the words you want to hear,
"Lord, you are all that I hold dear."

Often, Lord, I've given time
And riches for the sons of thine,
My treasures, talents giv'n away,
Toiled for you a long hard day.

But deep inside I trust you not,
I trust in riches that will rot
I trust the power of the mind
And all position I can find.

I've built my house on sinking sand,
Then mourn for tumult in my land.
Down low I sink in deep despair
When my foundations turn to air.

D. P. Myers

Now take my life and tear it down
And build it new in holy town,
A town that rests on solid rock,
You've with your blood built block by block.

Build house anew with strong walls straight
And in it, Lord, teach me to wait,
To wait on you when storms are strong
And not for selfish power long.

Lord, never let me stay again
In house I've built with selfish sin,
But keep my feet in fortress sure
Where found is your salvation pure.

63

Cold night air and howling wind
Empty waste; in cave I'm pinned.
Foes pursuing through dry land,
Enemy with unjust hand.
Stomach growling, food long gone
Wineskins cracked and parched lips drawn—

Can I still rejoice in thee
And the love you've shown to me?
Mem'ries of you in the night
Awesome power, glory's light.
Can dry lips still sing your praise
While I wait for joyful days?

But those moments when your light
Enters dark cave, making bright,
In black hole where now I live
Praise of steadfast love I'll give.
Empty pangs will fade away,
Satisfied by you that day.

A New Song

Let the thoughts of glory then
Help me now in darkened den,
Help me through my deepest pains
While my enemy still reigns.
Help my longing heart to know
Heaven's presence here below.

64

Why do I forever hide
    And fear the wicked man,
When you for me strength provide
    To stand against their plan?

Why does my heart break in two
    When their false words I hear?
Why do I not trust in you
    That you'll be ever near?

Even though I know your love
    Is constant through all time,
It's so hard to rise above
    False accusation's grime.

How long must, O Lord, I live
    Within these prison walls?
How long to them will you give
    The keys that keep me small?

Break me free from dark restraints.
    Remove the evil guard
Whose false words have been constraints,
    A reputation marred.

D. P. Myers

But this man whom I've become
    With dark and brooding soul
Needs your love to overcome
    My heart's dark empty hole.

Then aloud your praise I'll sing,
    New songs will my life write.
To all men your glories ring
    Of how for us you'll fight.

Even though the fight is long
    I'll with your strength endure.
Then one day I'll sing the song
    Of all your vict'ries sure.

65

When rays so bright pierce darkest night,
    When you our sins forgive,
    When up from death we live,
Our waking eyes see glory's light
    And life to us you give.

The power of the mountain high,
    The valleys sweet below,
    The flower's smell I know,
From nothing these did you bring nigh
    And joy to us bestow.

The rolling of the raging sea,
    The fins that crest the wave,
    The urchins in dark cave,
Just like the fish in waters free
    I live because you gave.

A New Song

The stalwart trees that stand so proud,
    The canopy so fair,
    The peace that's under there,
And like this verdant leafy shroud,
    Love's cover do you share.

All fields holding meat and grain,
    All strong plants bearing fruit,
    All food that comes on root,
All ever fresh by gentle rain,
    Grace free through heaven's chute.

Your loving hands hold all you made,
    Your creatures great and small,
    Your image bearers all,
And then eternal life conveyed
    To those who heed your call.

66

Clear the whole earth sings your praise.
    Why do I not my voice raise?

By love's hand you've guided me.
    Why at times do I not see?

Blinded are these eyes of mine.
    Why blind to the glory thine?

I see not the path you made
    With bright light through midnight shade,

Through the heights when I am blessed
    Or the pits of my life messed.

D. P. Myers

I see not your holy hand
    Or how close to me you stand.

I see not your hand of love
    Offered in a stranger's glove.

Drop the scales from my eyes
    So I see not blinding lies.

Let me see that you are near
    And you hold me ever dear.

Then my voice will clearly fly
    To your throne above the sky,

And my lips will sing to men
    Of your holy works again.

67

Vast blessings do you pour on men,
    We often think them fine.
But evil is the heart that then
    Wants all them to be mine.

We spend them for desires vast,
    Our pleasures always soar,
And when we use them to the last
    We turn and ask for more.

But does it ever cross our mind
    These gifts are not for me?
I wonder if we'll someday find
    You've given them for thee?

A New Song

You give us gifts to share your name
    To all your peoples here,
To spread through all the earth your fame
    So all to you draw near.

We are a river, not a pond,
    Through us your gifts should flow.
And what you send should point beyond
    So you can all men know.

68

Through deserts you will lead
    Past enemy and foe,
And though at times I bleed,
    I trust that best you know.
    I follow where you go.

In lonely days I live
    With broken heart in pain,
Yet oft' to me you give
    A shelter from the rain,
    A place with you again.

And weak as I am now,
    Unable to defend,
Your strength will show me how
    To evil never bend,
    To stand until the end.

While mute may be my tongue,
    Not knowing what to say,
Into my heart that's wrung
    You pour your love each day.
    You show me a new way.

D. P. Myers

So on eternal morn
    When you I fin'lly see,
I will be newly born
    And freely sing of thee,
    And praise eternally.

69

False, O Lord, my ways have been
    Before those that I know,
Waiting in the dark till when
    Time would the hidden show.

False rock thrown in my life's pool,
    Broad ripples crashing wide,
Waves and breakers are your tool
    To push me to your side.

Just would be this storm of life
    To break my living hull,
But you chose instead of strife
    To issue mercy's call.

Surface that's been broken true,
    False ripples soon arise.
No wall can I build anew
    To shrink their damning size.

Truth I knew would soon come out,
    But must I bear false too?
Rocking now on waves of doubt,
    I question all I do.

A New Song

Cast about by phantom waves,
    I ask for your just hand
To calm storm and then to save
    And bring me to safe land.

On your hand that calms the sea
    Rests clearly one dark scar.
In a moment then I see
    A deep and unjust mar.

Hands unstained by sin and pure
    Bear guilty marks of mine.
Supreme mercy's act I'm sure
    When sins of mine are thine.

Help me, Lord, to ride each crest
    And all the troughs so deep,
Trusting that your plan is best
    To ever safe me keep.

And on rippled pond I ask,
    Please give me words to sing
Of your gracious saving task
    Till me to shore you bring.

70

How often I desire you
    Would speed your hand to save
And make my life now ever new
    And over troubles pave.

I want my life to now be sweet,
    My enemies to shame.
Lord, place them underneath your feet
    For glory of your name.

D. P. Myers

But patient I have never been
    When life produces pain.
My heart breaks, my voice cries, "Lord, When,
    When will you stop the rain?"

Yet rain and pain is your sweet touch
    To bring about the best,
And even though endure I much,
    All leads to your good rest.

So help me, Lord, on you to wait
    Your patience to me give.
And help me stand under life's weight
    And ever with you live.

71

Your salvation far and wide.
    Beyond my simple mind.
Beyond words and depths inside,
    Its edge I cannot find.

Since before first day of life,
    Before I drew a breath,
In me you worked good and strife
    To save me 'fore my death.

Often, Lord, my eyes are on
    The troubles of the day,
Not your saving hand upon
    Me all along life's way.

Open eyes to see the new
    Paths leading from hell's flame.
Open lips to sing of you
    Of my salvation's name.

A New Song

Let me not go to the grave
    Before the youth I tell
Of your many acts that save
    And pull me from sin's cell.

Let the generations see
    Your strong and holy tower
By the words you give to me
    Until life's final hour.

72

Eternal as your reign may be
    With might and strength far known,
The poor and needy you still see,
    You keep them as your own.

Lord over all, your rule still stands,
    Your enemies destroy.
And all the poor you hold in hand,
    Protection you employ.

Your holy name, your wondrous name
    Rings for the earth to hear
With power, glory, and all fame,
    All of your foes thus fear.

But when, O Lord, I want to ask
    Will justice be for all?
And when will men of evil task
    See holy judgment fall?

It seems the land both far and wide
    Are by the dark oppressed,
And those who cling unto your side
    Are evermore distressed.

D. P. Myers

The pain I see makes my heart faint,
    I know not what to do.
How can I help bring some restraint,
    Or must I wait on you?

How much new blood must there be spilled,
    Dark sands on far-off shores?
How many more men will be killed
    Till you say, "Nevermore!"

I want to trust that justice lives,
    Oppression soon to end.
But when will mercy's hand you give,
    And peace when will you send?

Lord, give me patience to trust long,
    Protect from unjust men.
And in this pain grant me a song
    Until you come again.

Responses to Book Three of the Psalms: 73 – 89

73

Long the days of sorrow and of tears,
Cloudy vision of my prior years.
Broken heart that oft' for mercy longs,
But dark days have muted my life-song.
O, from sin a moment to be free,
Dry my eyes then clearly could I see,

A New Song

Your good hand that works at holy pace,
Justice coming here in time and space.
Evil men through pride who stand so tall,
Righteous ones who ever grow so small.
Soon to find through justice order new,
Evil judged; the good stand tall with you.

With dry eyes this truth I clearly know.
Open lips tell how your love you show.
Yet even so, dark may seem my days,
And in pain I walk along life's ways.
Your good hand will leave me not alone,
Guiding me through life and to your throne.

74

It seems that through the years of man
And each day you have had a plan,
Yet I ask, "Where's the great I Am?"

The forces dark forever stand
Against your people in the land
Beyond the reach of your strong hand.

And often your good people hide
From evil's devastating tide
That wipes the righteous ones aside.

When will you come and help us all,
Defeating evil, standing tall,
Victory singing out your call?

Your help must ever come to me
To be as patient as can be
Until your coming, Lord, I see.

D. P. Myers

75

When shaking, Lord, I often run
    To powers I can see.
But on this earth there is not one
    With power like to thee.

You steady toppling kingdoms far
    And calm upheaval near.
Your plan includes the distant star
    And all on earth that's dear.

But still I fret when troubles mount,
    I trust what I can touch
And never go to crimson fount
    Where love flows ever much.

I scratch and claw the dirty ground
    And build an idol fair,
A god in whom is no life found—
    It's mute without a care.

At other times my trust I place
    In friends I've come to love,
But human love cannot replace
    The Father's holy dove.

It can't replace his mighty hand
    That strikes the evil foe
And brings his peace throughout the land
    To those that love him so.

Help me, my Lord, when troubles rise
    To trust in you alone,
And teach me, Lord, to raise my eyes
    Through trials to your throne.

76

How to fear the Lord's strong hand
    That seeks to do me good
When dark foes throughout the land
    Don't fear him as they should.

How audacious is their plan?
    They strive. They war. They kill.
Disrespecting every man
    Who seeks to do thy will.

Punishing your children far
    And wide and close to home,
Oft' I wonder where you are
    And why you let them roam.

Lord, I know some future day
    Your justice will cry out.
Why do you not show today
    That these men you will rout?

Lord, I find it hard to fear
    You when your works aren't seen.
Let me see that you are near
    With just and loving mien.

Let me know the wicked foes
    Are under your control
And your loving justice grows
    To make the broken whole.

Teach me how to fear a'right
    And live so you I please.
As you then for justice fight,
    I'll live down on my knees.

77

My heart breaks at midnight hour
    And hidden tears appear,
In my weak and dwind'ling power
    I want you ever near.

But silent heaven is my bed
    And lonely time my sheet
Like shrouds that cover one who's dead
    Who speaks this final bleat,

"Why ever do my troubles mount
    Like mound on fresh dug grave?
And why will you not them surmount
    And from death's battle save?

Why can't I see your works of old
    Flash on my mind's blank screen?
No strength or love did you withhold
    From those of righteous mien."

    "You must remember that my love
        Is not constrained by time.
    It ever flows from me above
        Perfectly and sublime."

"You know my eyes are not so clear,
    They're filled with selfish flow.
You know I can't see how you're near
    And that you love me so."

    "I want to show you what I've done
        Now and in days long past,
    And all the vict'ries I have won
        With my strong love steadfast.

A New Song

    I'll give you strength from my past ways
        And grant you night's sweet sleep,
    Then in your dark and lonely days,
        I'll show that you I keep."

78

How does the man with mem'ry short
    Tell others what you've done,
The man who has no past report
    To show the paths you've run?

Is it mem'ry that has failed?
    Just maybe it's his eyes.
With holy sight darkly veiled
    He misses heaven's skies.

He disconnects your active hand
    From tools that you have used,
And so your movement in the land
    With nature is confused.

And thus, no stories he can tell
    Of your redeeming ways,
He misses sight of Spirit's swell
    Beneath him all his days.

I often find myself like him,
    Not seeing how you move.
As over time my sight grows dim,
    Your hand so hard to prove.

Lift the veil that blinds my sight
    And let me see you there,
How through the years your guiding light
    Was with me ever'ywhere.

D. P. Myers

79—First Response[5]

Bleating, snarling, sheepish wolf,
Sinful bliss from wool to hoof,
Never finding comfort in
Hairy or a wooly skin.

Angels, demons, in and out,
Love and hate and spies and scouts,
Places dark and lands of light,
Working out the inner fight.

Hellish heaven steps and end
Heart and head around each bend,
Tug and tussle night and day
Till my life's eternal way.

Will wolf or sheep win the war?
Bleating, snarling, whining roar.
Blood will drip, and tear will fall.
Tell me which one will stand tall.

---

[5] There are a number of Psalms to which I have written multiple poetic responses. I have included a few so that the reader might see how approaching the same psalm at different times can result in varying responses.

A New Song

79—Second Response

Slowly do you draw the bow
    While enemies advance,
When you'll shoot we long to know

Wall's protection tumbles down,
    My foes are passing near.
Where are you, Lord of renown

Stones and threats they hurl high,
    They mock your holy name.
Will you come 'fore death is nigh

We, your sheep, await your hand
    To punish all our foes.
Will you come and save your land

Someday soon your steadfast love
    Will purge the wicked soul.
Then our praise will rise above,
    For you make all things whole.

D. P. Myers

80

It is your hand that plants
    that nurtures and that feeds.
It is your breath that blows
    with life that I so need.
And, Lord, you are the one
    that pulls out all the weeds.
Why does it then seem like
    you from me do recede?

I know that my past choices
    were once all filled with strife.
I know my evil nature
    with sin full it is rife.
But Lord, for how much longer
    will you squeeze tight my life?

My Lord, I know that ev'ry day
    with passions dark I fight,
And yet despite my sinful ways,
    I long for your bright light.

Now from the dead, Lord, please me raise
    So through my life your name I'll praise.

A New Song

81

How often have I filled my ears
    With pleasures and with things
And thus have lost too many years
    Your songs I did not sing.

I used to hear your voice speak clear
    And follow in your ways,
Your presence seemed so very near
    And with me every day.

But when dark pleasures became dear
    My hearing was impaired,
Your holy voice became unclear
    And my heart's love was shared.

A heart that shares its love appears
    To be so rich indeed.
But to be true its nerves are seared
    And love turns into need.

And what was once a loving tear
    Shed for the heart of God
Has turned into a selfish fear
    Of losing idol's fraud.

Lord, silence all the empty cheer
    With its loud din raised high,
And in the quiet let me hear
    Your holy loving sigh.

D. P. Myers

82

Do I judge unjustly
And trample on the poor?
Do the poor ones trust me
To on them mercy pour?

You have given power
Position to your sons
In this life's short hour,
Then to the grave we run.

But till our life's last sign
When under we will go,
We are your loving vine
To help the weak and low.

For it is only grace
Poured from your holy throne
That lets us see your face
And calls us all your own.

There is no work I do
To earn your gift of love,
It flows down ever new
From crimson lamb above.

So from deep gratitude
To others I should give
Out of my plentitude
To help other men live.

83

Why do I seek for justice
    on my enemies' head?
Why do I long for your name
    to cover them with dread?
But when the foes aren't outward
    but within me instead,
Would still I want your strong hand
    to strike my foes all dead?

I have often been oppressed
    by dark and evil hand.
I know I've become outcast
    at home in my sweet land.
But when the trouble's over,
    I still want tall to stand,
Proclaiming loud your good name
    and mercy that is grand.

I am constantly aware
    of my dark sin each day,
And that my unique demons
    pursue me on life's way.
Often they will shut my heart
    till nothing I can say,
But, Lord, I'm asking won't you,
    please cast them all away.

And while my foes still haunt me
    my head drops low in shame,
My voice long clear is muted
    And I don't speak your name,
Each day that I find dawning
    is ever dark the same.
Please won't you give me freedom
    so your name I'll proclaim?

D. P. Myers

Lord, help me lift my head high
    as long for me you fight,
And then when they are all gone
    I'll stand in your sweet light—
Steadfast love renewing me
    so in you I'll delight—
Forever with my tongue loosed
    I'll sing long of your might.

84

I hope someday
    to find myself
        in holy house of gold.
I hope someday
    to see your face,
        your beauty to behold.
I hope someday
    after the grave
        to hear your wisdom told.

But till that time
    I trust that you
        will walk with me each day.
And till that time
    I'll trust in you
        to ease life's painful way.
And till that time
    I'll trust your strength
        will help me not to stray.

A New Song

Now help me, Lord,
    to love your ways
        full in you to delight.
And help me, Lord,
    to love in pain
        when day has turned to night.
And let me, Lord,
    by your great love
        to see eternal light.

85

You've given all that I can ask,
    And then you've given more.
You've opened up your holy cask,
    And on me love doth pour.

But faithfulness is not my way,
    I often reject you.
And though you give me breath each day,
    I each day sin anew.

What putrid worm within my soul
    Whose passing leaves dark sin,
Rejects your love that makes me whole
    Then burrows deep again?

It burrows to the place I choose
    Where sinful passions thrive.
As every inch to him I lose—
    I falsely seem alive.

Behind him does my folly grow,
    False life that leads to death.
Then I in wretched tunnels know
    My only hope's your breath.

D. P. Myers

Your breath that blows the sin from me
    And gives to me new life,
And for a time I turn to thee
    Away from all my strife.

Then holy, pure, and righteous, I
    Walk daily on life's path.
My hope eternal lifted high,
    For you have stayed your wrath.

But even though your steadfast love
    Flows freely from your hand
And righteousness pours from above,
    My heart can't worm withstand.

If *can't* or *won't* I true know not,
    The worm within me lies.
It's digging deep to my heart's rot,
    Eternal soul's demise.

Don't stay your hand so long, my Lord,
    Please kill the filthy worm.
And then in me will be restored
    A faithfulness that's firm.

86

The guilt that comes along each day
    Arrives in many darkened ways.

At times it is the guilt of sin
    That rides so heavy on my skin.

At others there is deep regret
    Of time that I have poorly spent.

A New Song

Each day my burden seems to grow
    With sins that drop my visage low.

And nearly every state of shame
    Bears down its full force on my name.

Oh, that my sin would bring to me
    Remorse for what I've done to thee.

Then all my guilt and shame would move
    My heart to your forgiving love.

87

"This one was born there,"
Loud this cry rings true.
But not ev'ry heir
Is fully renewed.

For deep down inside
My soul's hidden cave
A dark spring resides
That waters my way.

And from the ground grows
Bent plants and bad fruit,
All fed by dark flow
From cavern to root.

Yet other wet beds
So brightly they run
From scars that have bled
Pure blood of the Son.

D. P. Myers

The large crimson drops
Turn dark into light,
And fetid flow stops
Stream turning so bright.

Oh, that my dark spring
To crystal would turn.
Then bent plants would bring
Fruit's joyful return.

88

Do I think that you will raise
Souls from death at end of days
From the grave to give you praise?

Do I think that now and here
My small life is to you dear
With my days so filled with fear?

Do I think that troubles all
From your throne upon me fall
So that to you I will call?

Do I like to be alone
In dark solitude to groan
Even though I'm called your own?

I have longed to have a friend
Staying with me till the end,
From the pit when I ascend.

Then the pain that's in my past—
Pain I thought would always last—
From me ever will be cast.

A New Song

And the days with troubles rife,
Insecurities, and strife
Will be gone from that new life.

So until when I'll be free
In this darkness that I see,
Won't you come and sit with me?

89

Even when you do me well
With your grace from high above
And your faithful steadfast love,
It's more help than I can tell,
Yet my life, it seems like hell.

Lord, I know you care for me
And my good you always seek,
And to others I should speak
Of your mercies that I see.
But my Lord, where might you be?

Groaning night and day my heart,
It is longing for your touch
And to be with you so much
And to never be apart.
When did you from me depart?

Lord, it seems you've staid your hand
And you left the evil man
To enact his wicked plan
And your servants you remand
To his will throughout this land.

D. P. Myers

Lord, when will your Spirit blow
Setting all the wrongs a'right,
Shining on us holy light
Warming us up in love's glow
So your justice then we'll know?

Lord, until such time, will you
Teach me how to sing your praise?
And my voice in hope to raise
Of all that I know you'll do
When all life you make anew.

Responses to Book Four of the Psalms: 90 – 106

90

My life I've spent in hiding
    My time has passed me by,
My secrets on me riding
    As years from me they fly.

But naught of my dark secrets
    I've hid from human eyes
Can live before your deepness,
    For in your light they die.

Yet in my darkened places
    I seek their friendship oft',
And wonder if your grace is
    Enough my soul to loft,

A New Song

To lift me from the dark pit
    Of muck and death and sin,
Leading me so far from it,
    This hellish life I'm in.

To search out your grand measure
    Through all my years and days
And find no greater pleasure
    Than seeking all your ways.

Then be taken one day home,
    The castle of the King,
Where your glories will be shown
    And sinner cleansed will sing.

91

Where else can I go
    for comfort in my pain,
    avoid the terror's reign,
    and live new life again?

Who else do I know
    with strength to conquer all,
    with love for great and small,
    who will not let me fall?

Is there else on earth
    that keeps me all my days,
    that guides me all my ways,
    who with me always stays?

Who else can I trust
    with fears that come at night,
    my shame seen in the light,
    who will for me still fight?

D. P. Myers

Where is such a one
    like him so high above,
    with Son who showed great love,
    who sends to me his dove?

92

Many days when I awake
    My work is all I see.
Focus does from me then take
    My eyes away from thee.

Through the pane I see the wood,
    Tree's canopy above,
And on grassy blanket good
    Stands creatures made in love.

Songs from beaks filling the air,
    They echo your sweet word,
Bringing life to all that's fair,
    My heart with longing stirred.

Deep and great must be the one
    Whose words brought forth this land,
Giving life through shining sun
    To all creation grand.

More than earth has his hand wrought
    In dirt his image placed,
And for souls he long has fought
    To see us face to face.

But from pane my eye averts
    To tasks that fill each day.
In such times your joy deserts,
    I focus on my way.

Yet in bed I lay at night
>   Long after work is done,
Slowly then my thoughts take flight
>   To mercies of the Son.

93

Beauty drapes over your throne
>   Strength and power are your own.
>> Holiness to us you've shown.

Land of beauty brings delight
>   Wild nature shows her might.
>> Holy word gives us new light.

Nature's force beyond compare—
>   Water, earth, and even air.
>> Holy word lays nature bare.

Only you can beauty give
>   Nature's power you outlive.
>> Holy laws will ever live.

Beauty of this land is vast,
>   By your word has it been cast.
>> Holy word from first to last.

Holy pure ever are you—
>   Mercies to us daily new.
>> Holiness will all renew.

Holiness surpasses all,
>   Strength and beauty 'fore it fall,
>> And by it bent men stand tall.

D. P. Myers

94

How oft' the world's weight I bear
    And all my troubles keep?
I never pain with others share
    And long my soul does weep.

At times I seek a numbing salve
    In work throughout the day,
But peace my soul it does not have
    In this numb lonely way.

The strife that covers all the land,
    The friends that I have lost,
I try to right with my own hand
    But pay a futile cost.

Injustice everywhere I look
    From home to farthest shore,
The earth's foundations have been shook,
    How, Lord, can there be more?

And so my soul, Lord, bears this weight,
    My gaze cast to the ground,
Will lonely struggle be my fate?
    Where can relief be found?

I cry for justice on the earth,
    Repay the wicked man!
Such pain they have all been from birth,
    O Lord, what is your plan?

But in my rage against the dark
    I hear a still small voice,
A voice in dark like tiny spark,
    "Like you, they've made a choice.

A New Song

They may have chosen darkened path
    Bringing the earth its pain,
But you have chosen inner wrath,
    Hatred, and lonely strain.

I've always only wanted you
    To bring to me your fears,
Your pains, and all your burdens too
    And let me dry your tears.

Your shoulders strong as they may be,
    Such weight weren't meant to bear.
The word to flesh was born for thee,
    Your burdens now to share.

So let my words your heart console
    And all your burdens take,
Relinquish to me all control
    And of my joy partake!"

You know I want to give it all,
    These weights and pains of mine.
Lord, free my grip on great and small
    To rest in love divine.

95

Am I content to merely praise
    Your work throughout the land?
And will I only to you raise
    New songs of your great hand?

I'll sing how you've made mountains fair
    And valleys far below,
The mighty waves that spray the air,
    The earth I so well know.

D. P. Myers

The stoic trees and mighty falls,
    The flowers in the plain—
Lord, by your strength you've made them all,
    I sing to you again.

Though when I often see the trees
    And want to stand and sing,
It doesn't drive me to my knees
    Or to you worship bring.

I take all nature's beauty in,
    Yet it can't change my heart.
It's easy to live deep in sin
    And love your nature's art.

But only when my knee I bend
    And place my trust in you,
Rebellion in my heart will end,
    My life will you renew.

So simple is it to stand straight
    In love with nature's show,
But hard to humble self and wait
    With head and heart bowed low.

Lord, let my eyes see nature's sign
    You've painted onto space
So that my focus realigns
    From sign unto your face.

A New Song

96

How many are the songs to sing
    Of how your nature's beauty rings?

Already many have been sung
    The bells of beauty have been rung.

Yet all the beauty that I see
    Is but a shadow cast by thee.

This finite earth and space above
    Are darkened spots cast by your love.

The trees, the plains, the mountains grand
    Are naught compared to your strong hand.

The leaf, the grass, the flower small
    Are hints of new life for us all.

But songs of beauty that are near
    Turn quickly old—that's what I fear.

That even though these songs are true,
    They're old, for they sing not of you.

They sing not of your sacrifice
    And how you rescue men from vice.

They sing not of eternal God
    Nor how you help men through life plod,

Nor the Spirit's holy fire
    Lifting lowly souls up higher.

They only sing of nature's ways
    But not you of the ancient days.

D. P. Myers

The songs you want my voice to lift
    Are of your great salvation gift,

New songs of how you make men pure
    And of your steadfast love that's sure,

New songs with words of righteousness
    And songs that sing of holiness.

Lord, help me sing eternal verse
    Before all men your love rehearse.

97

If nature trembles at your call
And 'fore your throne all knees will fall,
Then why can I not give my all?

If joyfully the coastlands sing
And glory from the mountains ring,
Then why can I not my song bring?

Lord, why does evil spark in me
A wicked longing filled with glee
Not a will to bend my knee?

In evil heart I need your light
To banish darkness from my sight
So I in goodness will delight.

And then before your holy throne
I'll stand with those you call your own
With joyful heart and sins atoned.

98

Open my eyes that I might see
>   Your present working hand,
For I have found I'm blind to thee
>   Your work throughout the land.

I see injustice all around,
>   The good suppressed by bad,
And groaning earth, I hear its sound,
>   It seems that all's gone mad.

Like Martha, Lord, I know one day
>   You'll triumph o'er the grave,
But all in present troubled way,
>   I'm not so sure you'll save.

Is this a land without your love
>   And your salvation's touch,
Or am I blind to you above
>   And to your loving clutch?

Open my eyes to see you move
>   And let my voice cry out
A song, my Lord, that you approve
>   To wipe away all doubt.

Yes, free my voice that I may sing
>   A song to you that's new
About salvation that you bring
>   Pointing all back to you.

Lord, let me sing new songs out loud,
>   New verses to construct,
And sing them 'fore the earth's great crowd,
>   And of your love instruct.

D. P. Myers

99—First Response

All praises sung unto the Lord
    His power told to all.
His truth and justice I adore
    Before his throne I fall.

His words proclaimed across the land,
    His justice will I tell,
But not before I praise the hand
    That will all evil fell.

A song anew is sung on high,
    A verse of mine rings clear.
Up to his throne our words must fly,
    Then to those who are near.

99—Second Response

The Lord's power seems to be
    Far removed from you and me.

Sitting high upon his throne,
    Might and justice are his own.

We must then before him fall
    If "our Lord" we wish to call.

But he's not a distant God
    From his creatures that are flawed.

He speaks loving words to man,
    Leading us by holy plan,

A New Song

Keeping us from sinful path,
    Guarding from eternal wrath.

Mercy, justice hand in hand
    As he walked upon this land.

Raising dead men from the grave
    From sin's penalty to save.

Living voice to you I sing,
    Raised to you, my God, my King.

100—First Response

I went to church to find the Lord,
    Instead I found my friends,
      And sat upon the pew with them
And found that I was bored.

I looked around at wall and spire,
    I listened to the Word.
    I thought about the day ahead
And found no holy fire.

I think I erred in knowing where
    To look to find the Lord.
    I sat below the lofty roof
And said my prayer there,

But he is not within the space
    To which I weekly go—
    Both friends and walls they merely point
Beyond to holy face.

D. P. Myers

100—Second Response

Basic truths are filled with gold,
    My head tells me it's true.
Yet my longing heart is bold
    To want great signs from you.

Move the mountains, banish foes,
    Cure all my friend's deep pain.
In my desert make life grow
    And don't send me life's rain.

When great signs I do not see,
    Depression settles in.
How can I more selfish be
    To wonder where you've been?

Often I forget your hand
    Has brought me forth from dust,
And you lead me through life's land,
    You only can I trust.

When I stumble and then fall—
    So often ev'ry day—
Steadfast love to me does call
    In ever-faithful way.

Maker's hand, Redeemer's love
    How can I want much more
Than to enter courts above
    And praise you evermore?

101

Blameless ways I want to ponder
As through life my feet far wander.

But I wander weak and weary
Through my failures ever teary.

Blurry eyes ever obscuring
Holy ways that are alluring.

Ever drawn to righteous pathway,
Never wanting to go halfway.

Always seeking good to follow
Not a wicked life that's shallow.

Never shallow but so deeply
Rich rewards never come cheaply.

Costly is the grace he's given,
Freely all my sins forgiven.

Paying all, my tears he's drying,
Righteous ways now freely trying.

Freely walking pathways holy,
Burdened not by things so lowly.

Someday then to heaven wander,
Ever holy face to ponder.

D. P. Myers

102

This painful life,
    these shortened days,
        the troubles that I know—
My stumbling feet
    and shattered dreams,
        your blessings ebb and flow.

All that I am
    compared to you
        like falling autumn's leaf—
My painful times
    and triumphs all,
        a life that is so brief.

But still I sound
    barbaric yawp
        for all those yet to live,
To know you love
    small ones like me
        and freely grace you give.

For you are strong,
    eternal life,
        unchanging throughout time,
So by your grace
    and steadfast love
        from life's dark pit we climb.

My future hope,
    eternal home,
        this earth you throw away.
Your children all
    raised up by you
        to your eternal day.

A New Song

103—First Response

Your love fills up the heavens
    It falls upon the earth,
But in the house I live in
    All that I know is dirt.

My hands are darkly blackened
    My fingers claw for light,
And in this muck I'm planted
    Your love seems out of sight.

Perhaps I've built a shelter
    Of darkness for my sin.
Perhaps I've shunned the helper
    Who wants to come within.

When ever will you break through
    My dingy shelter's walls,
Washing off the residue
    Of ugly sinful scrawls?

Will bloody hands be lowered
    To lift me from this hole?
Will loving words be showered
    To cleanse and make me whole?

103—Second Response

Short are the days of trouble.
    Winds eternal blow.
    All's wood, hay, stubble.

Golden buds and verdant grass
    At the end of days,
    They will fade and pass.

D. P. Myers

Hopeless seem our lifelong dreams,
    Holding ever tight
    To temporal streams.

Finite life moves ever fast
    Filled with work of mine,
    Work that will not last.

Coming down from high above,
    Holiness poured out
    Brings his steadfast love.

He redeems and renews man,
    Work that will not end
    In our time's short span.

Blessings make my soul rejoice,
    Lifting up on high
    My forgiven voice

To praise, sing, and bless the Lord
    For his saving grace
    Given by his Word.

104

When I look through windowpane
    of dust and humid dew,
Nature's glory and your strength
    come barely shining through.

Muddled forms of stately trees
    like colored shadows stand
Under shroud of earthly haze
    that covers all the land.

A New Song

Land that on you waits each day
    for food and water dear,
Evidence through nature's ways
    that you are always near.

Near, you stand in happy times
    and with us you rejoice,
Also in our weary days
    when lonely cries our voice.

Many are the days I wait
    while downcast is my soul.
When will foggy pane be cleaned
    and vision become whole?

When will dust and humid dew
    be cleaned so I can see
Through the beauty of the earth
    your steadfast love for me?

Oft' I ask, Lord, where you are
    when cast down ever low.
Long I look through what you've made
    to see your glory show.

May you ever clean the panes
    that darken my soul's eyes,
Every morning till that day
    when I see heaven's prize.

Morning's light will pierce the fog
    and lift away the shroud,
Street of gold leading on high
    filled with a holy crowd.

D. P. Myers

Journey from this shadow land
    to colors strong and bright,
And to holy city go
    to find the source of light.

Throne of glory's light shines out
    before it we then sing
New song brought to you in joy
    your blessings ever ring.

105—First Response

Voices high must lifted be,
Praise and glory sung to thee.
Deeds of old and works anew,
Mercies in the morn' like dew
On the grass of faithful lives
O'er the time of pain and strife.
Through our pain your glories sing.
Through our flaws we praise the king.
Others 'round may hear our song,
Others lost may seek and long,
Long for springs in deserts dry
And for hands to dry the eye.
Song that's lifted high to you
Tells the earth of life anew.

105—Second Response

In stately halls your pictures stand,
Each painted by your loving hand.
Your acts of mercy framed in wood,
Retelling all your works of good.

A New Song

Some statues carved in forms of man
Who carried out your holy plan.

A golden floor and marble wall,
Your strength and glory seen by all.
Hung up high are tales of pain
And struggles through dark nights of rain.
Famine, exile, prison too,
In hope the pris'ners wait for you.

A wooden manger stands alone
Recalling where your glory shone—
A cross, a tomb, a linen fold,
Through death to life your story told.
Beyond the linen fold there sits
Twelve men with flames, the last portraits.

Long do these stately halls go on,
But paintings on the walls are gone.
Yet people through the halls still walk
And of the missing art still talk.
They seem to see what is not there.
They stop. They point. They look. They stare.

At first I thought these people odd,
Pretending at some art to nod,
But as I wandered through halls long
Past missing art and wand'ring throng,
I wondered if my eyes were blind
Or if I was just dim of mind.

How can I see your hist'ry past,
Those works you've done that long will last,
But still not see your present art,
The work that shows how you impart
To men that live in modern day
Protection all along life's way,
And how the people you still guide

D. P. Myers

Through pain and joy while at their side?
You've given me my eyes to see
Your glory worked in history,
But now, O Lord, I want to know
Your current work so I can show
To those who after me will live
That you have never stopped to give
Yourself, your Son, your Spirit's love
To us below, down from above.

106

Why do I forget
    the pleasure of your ways?
Why must I regret
    my wicked evil days?

Long your steadfast love
    has faithful ever been
Freely from above
    your covenant with men.

Yet my fickle heart
    will follow sinful whim.
From you I depart
    down pathways ever grim.

How can you stand by
    and let me run so far?
O, how must you cry
    when oft' your hands I scar.

When away I run,
    I do not, Lord, know how
I forget your Son,
    his bloodied beaten brow.

A New Song

Yet you never leave
    nor do you me forsake.
Though you still I grieve,
    you always me retake.

Will I ever sing
    your praises for all time?
Will I ever ring
    a loud and grateful chime?

Your love I recall,
    your ever-faithful hand,
Then to tell to all
    who live throughout the land.

Blessings do you give
    to all who heed your voice,
Ever with you live
    and ever to rejoice.

Responses to Book Five of the Psalms: 107 – 150

107

Have I been the hungry
    longing for a home?
Have I been the rebel
    far from God to roam?
Have I been in trouble
    seeing painful days?
Or have I been the fool
    chasing sinful ways?

D. P. Myers

I think I've been them all
    during my short life.
The choices that I make
    often lead to strife.
And even though I run
    far with wicked heart,
I've learned so long to play
    fake my holy part.

I know he's always seen
    through my cheap façade.
In love he punished me
    with his steadfast rod.
Yet out he reached his hand
    to my tremb'ling soul,
He pulled me close to him
    making my life whole.

I'm not the only one
    that he wants to hold—
All sheep across the land,
    drawing to his fold,
Calling to the needy
    and those close to death,
To the fool and troubled,
    giving Spirit's breath.

As my days grow shorter,
    stumbling, still I fall.
He patiently awaits
    for my troubled call.
Then up he raises me
    in this life I know,
As he ever always
    love for me will show.

108

Though battles rage and foes surround,
Deep in my heart there is a sound.

A single note that's barely heard
That grows in strength fed by your Word.

The note rings clear throughout my soul
When I am broken or am whole.

At times this note I barely hear.
At times this note is held so dear.

And there are times this note I hide,
Held in a prison deep inside.

In lonely cage it barely rings,
Reminding me that I should sing.

But in those times there barges in
A symphony outside my skin

With notes of glory over all,
With notes that make the little tall.

These notes oft' tear the cage apart
And free the song within my heart.

They move my lips in joyous song,
A song of love heard by earth's throng.

Yet there are times my heart is weak,
And bare comes from me a little squeak.

I mute the song you've brought from me
And then am silent as can be.

D. P. Myers

Lord, keep my heart from these foul moods
When I am silent, sit, and brood.

And when I mute my one true voice,
The only way I can rejoice

To sing of your great steadfast love
That faithfully comes from above.

This song is why you did me make.
So Lord, my dead soul please awake.

The prison doors in me break down
So I can then sing of your crown.

A song in me formed by your hands
To far be heard throughout the land.

109

Tearful cries unto the Lord
    Are covered by my sin.
Broken voice declares his Word
    While darkness reigns within.

For years I've taught of glory
    Before the young and old.
For years I've lived a story
    Of darkness never told.

A struggle ever keeping
    Me walking on this path
Between the joy I'm speaking
    And inner hate and wrath.

A New Song

Hopeful ev'ry day I start
    A clean and empty slate,
But like weeds within my heart
    Rise both lust and hate.

The weedy battle rages.
    It rips apart my soul.
It's torn so deep for ages
    To parts what once was whole.

I find I'm barely able
    To see his holy face,
And when I'm at his table
    I sit in low disgrace.

My inner battlefield
    Whereon this war is fought
Awaits to whom I'll yield
    In word and deed and thought.

I long for heaven's pleasure.
    I long for arms of love.
I want corroded treasure
    That lies not high above.

Will a confession save me?
    Will love of his I take?
Or will the battle daily
    My will at last it break?

Will he accept me broken?
    Will he look past my sin?
Or has my fate been spoken
    Since I keep giving in?

D. P. Myers

Can such a sinful person
    In love be held by him?
Or will this vile vermin
    Be doomed to darkness grim?

I know that the true answer
    To questions that I have
Is that his love's a banner,
    His crimson blood a salve.

I know his love's unbridled,
    Steadfast, and faithful too.
Salvation is unrivaled
    In making all men new.

I know that when I stumble
    And fall along life's way,
I only then must humble
    Myself and to him pray.

And through this long, long battle
    Against foe in and out
And in this constant struggle,
    I'll wait his vict'ry shout.

His shout that clears the field
    Of those who seek my shame,
And then they all will yield
    And bow before his name.

But until that time I'll sing
    And write of him new songs,
Broken life I'll daily bring
    To him my whole life long.

A New Song

110

I look around and see the pain
The world's troubles and the strain.
I wonder when you'll come to reign
And of this earth make new again.

The kings of far, the rulers near,
Decisions made producing fear.
The poor cry out, "When will you hear?
Oppressed we are from year to year!"

"I came not just for them," you say,
"I came to bring a better day,
A day when sin inside won't stay
And you can walk on holy way."

Your goals I think I understand—
To clean the heart and purge the land
Then ruling all with priestly hand,
But foes of mine I can't withstand.

Lord, let me last through life's dark night
And see my foes fall to your might.
Then see the dawn of kingdom's light
Beatific vision, holy sight!

111

I praise you, Lord, for what you do.
Your hand's great works are ever new—

The mountains high, the valleys low,
Your strength to man you ever show.

D. P. Myers

But grace you've poured out on my sins
Is where your greatest work begins.

For nature's scars in time will mend,
But human scars have hellish end.

This heart of mine so prone to fall
Cannot its own sin e'er forestall.

In tiny space, in dark of night,
My sinful self begins its fight.

It reaches, grabs, expands its reign
Till soul is marred with wicked pain.

Scarred soul then animates my limbs,
And I in darkness ever swim.

I reach and grab for passion's goal,
Corroded treasures tear my soul.

But life so marked by sinful brand
Is ever purged by crimson hand.

My scars the crimson hand will bear.
New life to me then it will share.

I praise you, Lord, for what you've done
Forever co-heir with your Son.

112

Do I fear you, Lord?
    Do I love your Word?
Will I change my life
    To match what I've heard?

Will I view your Word
    Through another lens—
Culture or hist'ry,
    My feelings or friends?

And if such a lens
    I place on my eyes,
How then can I see
    He who for me died?

How then will my eye
    Find truths that will last?
For all that I'm told
    Is changing so fast.

But first unto last
    Your Word does not change,
Your truth for my wants
    I cannot exchange.

So while all is change,
    Lord, help me to know
Immutable truth
    And love's steadfast flow.

And teach me to know
    The fear of the Lord
That to me will bring
    Eternal reward.

D. P. Myers

113

Voices clear sing loud on high,
    Angelic sounds are heard.
To your throne close we draw nigh
    With ev'ry loving word.

High above all on your throne
    Creation you survey.
To all below are you known
    In nature's full display.

But your heart you do not hide,
    You love to help the poor.
Them you lift and bring inside
    Your ever-open door.

Homeless and the barren too,
    You evermore will love.
Ev'ry morning mercies new
    To them from you above.

Yet I wonder if I break
    Your heart when I sing songs,
But no effort then I make
    To love who don't belong.

Praise is done in word and deed
    Or else our love is dead.
When we love all those in need
    We praise your thorn-crowned head.

114—First Response

From bondage dark are we taken
    To lands afar we go,
Where our sinful chains are broken,
    Your power makes it so.

Along life's road you lead me down
    Past mountains and the sea,
Past deep dark pits it winds around
    And streams dried up for me.

Yet all my steps aren't in the light,
    Some paths I tread with pain.
But trust in you is ever right
    Even with sinful stain.

Often though are my thoughts double
    Even when in your Word.
Still I wait for when soul's trouble
    Is cleft by your sharp sword.

How long until the darkness falls
    And your light shines within,
And till your glory cleanses all
    Removing all my sin?

The path away from bondage chains
    Is not an easy one,
But by your gentle hand's sweet pains
    I'll walk it with your Son.

D. P. Myers

114—Second Response

The seas that rage within my heart,
    The rivers in my soul,
The mountains and the valleys start
    Until they are made whole.

From prison did he free my life,
    My chains he broke away.
This life which once was full of strife,
    He's making new each day.

And though my broken heart rebels
    Against his loving hand,
The part that's clean to soiled tells,
    "Still follow his command."

Life's path ahead will be a fight,
    My soul the battle prize.
So patient must I walk in light,
    Led by his loving eyes.

115

The living trunk now dead,
    A static slice of life.
Its marrow has been bled
    By ax and saw and knife.

A moment caught in time,
    A figure carved in wood,
A slice of life divine,
    Eternal in its mood.

A New Song

Placed high upon a shelf
    For all around to see,
Its glory in itself,
    It points not unto thee.

The truth the form has missed
    Is that life always grows,
And that which once was is
    A life anew to know.

All mortal life we find
    Flows from the one above,
His life that lies behind
    All nature that we love.

Yet mortal life is not
    The same as life on high,
Each day our lives are fraught
    With changing nature's sigh.

But nature holds on tight
    To changeless deity,
His coalescing light
    With always more to see.

Beauty never ending,
    His mysteries unbound.
Story always moving,
    New truth is ever found.

These icons of my mind
    Hold nothing to his form.
Eternity will find
    New glories evermore.

D. P. Myers

116

Trapped so tight within a snare,
    Diseased and rotting soul,
I feed my heart with stagnant fare.
    I try to fill a hole.

I cry, but sin has muted tongue,
    My voice it cannot rise.
All words from me my sin has wrung
    And silenced my heart's cry.

Dark grievous tears are rolling down,
    My voice fails to speak,
And in such tears I soon may drown,
    For I am ever weak.

I have no way to find release
    From this pit long I've known.
My wicked ways I cannot cease
    Myself I can't dethrone.

Unless your hand you offer me,
    Your ears to me incline.
Unless you lift me to be free,
    I'll die in sin of mine.

Will gently then you dry my tears
    And wipe my guilt away?
And can you take my doubting fears
    That drove me from right way?

If so, then freely will I sing
    Of mercy you have shown,
And to your throne will then I bring
    My heart that you have known.

A New Song

You've known my heart from before time
    And how it's meant for you.
You've known I'd fall into sin's slime,
    Yet me you still renew.

So let my voice sing loud and long
    To those across the land,
And let me join the holy throng
    That moves by holy hand.

117

Love eternal,
    Love divine,
        Steadfast love,
Faithful through time—

Praise forever,
    Songs of love,
        From all men
To you above.

118

How often will you hear my cry
    And save me from distress,
And tolerate my life's great lie
    And clean up my life's mess?

How often can I come to you
    When into sin I've gone?
How often will you make me new
    With punishment withdrawn?

D. P. Myers

Will still you let me trust your hand
    To keep me from my foes?
And will you lead me to your land
    When sin within me grows?

I long for you to be my strength,
    For I am weak indeed.
In struggles through life's breadth and length
    Your help I ever need.

My foes I cannot battle long
    Before I fall in sin,
Then if to you I still belong,
    Such question burns within.

But even in my darkened state,
    I know your saving grace
Will wipe my sins from dirty slate
    When held in love's embrace.

So, Lord, into my dismal days
    When sins I often fight,
Let holy Word shine clear its rays
    My darkened path to light.

And let my tongue bring forth your praise,
    Your steadfast love to sing.
New songs to you through all my days
    Forever to you bring.

A New Song

119—Aleph[6]

The joyful romp of floppy ears
    Through grass of green and gold,
A just reward for all the years
    I've held the laws you told
To man so high upon the mount
    And all who stood below.
But oft' my sinful thoughts surmount,
    And shame will bring me low.
Oh, that my ways may always be
    True to what you've given,
So in this life I'll walk with thee
    And then with you in heaven.

119—Beth

Desire's chains will drag me down
    To depths so cold and dark.
The caves and holes of low renown
    Leave on my soul a mark.

From such places my earnest pleas
    Seem never more to fly.
They've lost their wings to go to thee
    And in the depths they die.

---

[6] Psalm 119 in the book of Psalms is written in an acrostic form and divided into twenty-two stanzas each containing eight verses with each verse in each stanza beginning with the successive letters of the Hebrew alphabet. Instead of writing one poem for the entire chapter, I chose to write a poem for each stanza. While I have not utilized the acrostic form in my poems, I have retained the Hebrew letter designation corresponding to the specific stanza in Psalm 119 for which the poem was a response.

D. P. Myers

I'm haunted by lost time and chance
    That sin has ripped from me,
And by the sense I've lost your glance,
    Alone on life's dark sea.

Yet in the dark I seek the way
    To find release from sin,
To prop my heart with heaven's stay
    That lets your light within.

But as the dogs return to wretch,
    I find my paths will tread
To places where my soul will fetch
    The pabulum of the dead.

The food on which my dark soul feeds
    Is found upon my shelves,
And yet I know the food I need
    Comes from the Word yourself.

Please guide me as I walk life's path
    To evermore you seek,
And keep my steps from sin and wrath
    As I am very weak.

119—Gimel

The battle rages ev'ry day,
My thoughts consumed in ev'ry way.
Which way is right? Help me, I pray.
Lord, will my choice be hell to pay?

Your words were given long ago,
The straightened paths for me to know,
But as I read and study so,
My dark desire stronger grows.

A New Song

Do I hide beneath desire,
Giving into deepest fire?
Can you make my sin retire,
Pulling me from filthy mire?

I'll lose my friends and comfort sure
If to this path my feet inure
While reaching for the sweet allure.
Will such a choice then hell secure?

I read your Word and turn the page,
Your laws and precepts do not age,
Yet still inside me sin does rage.
Please break me from my nature's cage.

Will you your goodness in me plow?
Then verdant plants will you allow
To crowd the thistles that stand now
That once were on your bloody brow?

119—Daleth

It's odd how tasty evil
    can often seem to be,
Engorging self primeval
    the darkest dreams in me.

My steps grow ever softer
    the longer that I hold
To ways I shouldn't wander
    far seeking for false gold.

The false joy often lifting
    me up to lofty heights,
My feet then barely touching
    the earth in rapture's flight.

D. P. Myers

But when the truth comes dawning
    like sun on foggy land,
I see in human longing,
    a phantom that now stands.

My substance slowly fading
    and dark dreams held so dear,
My longing quickly making
    of joy a salty tear.

Yet even in this trading
    of true for falsely thin
And in this slow unmaking
    of solid soul within,

I struggle to acknowledge
    the path I'm walking down
Is tread with the full knowledge
    of destiny's dark town.

Lord, make my soul now heavy
    with sorrow for my sin
And help me now live worthy
    of changes made within.

Please take my phantom substance
    and bring it back to earth,
Then with your holy utt'rance
    breathe life and give new birth.

Make me a solid creature
    that walks along your way,
A man with holy features
    now clearer ev'ry day.

A New Song

Then hand in hand, my Savior
    lead me along life's path
And quell this constant waver
    and keep me from your wrath.

119—He

I know your Word,
    though not complete.
Your wisdom flows
    to guide my feet.

Yet still my heart
    dark passions sway,
They draw my eyes
    another way.

It seems as I
    strengthen my mind,
My passions grow
    evil I find.

Then walking down
    this path of sin,
My cries to you
    stay deep within.

And rising up
    from my dark soul,
False pleasure's joy
    it takes a toll.

My voice is lost,
    no more to sing
And no more praise
    to you I bring.

D. P. Myers

Avert my eyes
    and draw my heart.
Let me begin
    with a new start.

Teach me your Word,
    your wisdom give,
On new paths walk,
    right with you live.

Teach me to love
    your precepts all,
And keep me from
    a sinful fall.

119—Waw

Clearly does the bird's song ring,
Always knowing what to sing.
Ne'er a thing can stifle tongue.
Joyful tune from him is sung.

But man's voice is not like theirs,
Heart and tongue exist in pairs.
When your laws our hearts don't love,
Voice cannot lift praise above.

When I walk on wicked path,
Leading to eternal wrath,
Truly truth I cannot speak
'Fore high kings or lowly meek.

Guard my heart each breaking day
So your truth I'll truly say.
Help me love your righteous law
So from lips truth won't withdraw.

Then like all creation's sound
On my lips will truth be found.
Ringing to the sons of men,
Truth I'll sing out once again.

119—Zayin

Do I truly hope
    in your words of life?
Do I rest in you
    in the midst of strife?

Does my anger rise
    when the wicked mock?
Do I comfort take
    in your Word, my Rock?

Is there any joy
    for me in your Word?
Is your law the source
    of my songs you've heard?

If I do not call
    on you in the night,
Do I then deserve
    to be made aright?

119—Heth

What sort of man when truth he sees
    Will turn his path around?
What sort of man then must he be
    Who seeks what can't be found?

D. P. Myers

These eyes of mine, they often gaze
    At passions found within.
Such hidden longings guide my ways
    To houses full of sin.

I am the man who often looks
    Away from holy words
And coldly pens my darkened book
    With steps that are absurd.

I follow ways of wicked men
    Their dark ropes will ensnare.
In prison then I wonder when
    I'll break these evil cares.

I look for truth around my feet.
    My hope falls empty back.
My lonely soul begins to weep
    For moorings that I lack.

But truth it comes not from the earth
    Nor from the heart of man,
It comes from lowly manger's birth
    By God's eternal plan.

119—Teth

Your Word is just.
My sin condemned.
I'm afflicted
Until life's end.

My path is hard,
But you are good.
Your steadfast love
Has always stood.

A New Song

But still I go
And leave your path,
Knowing I'll see
Your holy wrath.

Instead you give
Your hand of love.
Tears of mercy
Flow from above.

And through the years
When oft' I stray,
Your loving staff
Shows me the way.

Lord, help me now
To finish well
Then after life
With you to dwell.

119—Yodh

Ev'ry day my knowledge grows,
Wisdom's depths to ever know,
But my hope comes ever slow.

Before sin stands my weak heart
From your ways I oft' depart.
My life's pleasure falls apart.

Lonely and in pain I knew,
Hope was not in something true.
How I wish I'd trusted you.

D. P. Myers

Other trials there would be,
Life is never trouble-free,
But this guilt I would not see.

Thank you for your love steadfast
And new mercies that long last
And away you've not me cast.

Now, when in me sin is stirred,
Let me hope in what I've heard –
Spirit's voice throughout your Word.

And when then in you I trust
Not my dark and evil lust,
I'll rejoice for you are just.

Guide me now to love your ways,
Walking with you all my days,
Never far from holy gaze.

119—Kaph—First Response

Hanging dark and wrinkled,
    A wineskin in the smoke.
By the flames I'm crinkled,
    The coals my sins long stoke.

Hand is burnt by fire,
    It chars and scars my skin.
Still I hold desire,
    Temptations deep within.

How long will my heart hold
    To pain as dear as life?
When will I be so bold
    To banish all the strife?

Yet coming from without
    This fiery pit of mine
Strong hands that grasp and rout
    The dark to let light shine.

Then in the bottles high,
    In skins so dark and old,
He pours his holy sigh
    That warms my heart so cold.

Bringing to my darkness
    A life of light from him,
Showing me in weakness
    To cling to him, not sin.

119—Kaph—Second Response

Fire burning,
Wood smoking,
    rising
    wafting
        to the roof—

Bottle charring,
Leather cracking,
    sooty
    colored
        old wineskins—

Troubles coming,
Trials testing,
    clouding
    fogging
        sight of mine—

D. P. Myers

Heart retching,
Soul crying,
   cracking
   breaking
       in the night—

Word filling,
Love caressing,
   holding
   loving
       broken man—

119—Lamedh

Lonely have I wandered long,
Seeking places to belong
Round life's curve of ignorance,
Always hoping to find bliss.
Empty homes are constant found,
Lonely days devoid of sound.
Mournful cry within my soul,
Lonely heart an empty hole.
Friends I often fear to tell
Of pain deep and anguish swell,
Of eyes peering in my head,
Constant longing for the dead.
I am told through valley dark
Walks with me a saving ark,
Place of shelter from the storm,
Arms to hold me as I mourn,
Bed to rest from painful days,
Hands to guide along dark ways.
Grubby mitts these hands of mine,
Reaching for transcendent line.
Where are holy arms of love?

A New Song

Where is comfort from above?
Where is substance to hold near,
Ever close and ever dear?
Where's the touch, not phantom hope,
Hands to hold not faith to grope,
Not a promise far on high,
But a love that's to me nigh?
Will I ever happy walk
With a friend to hold and talk
Of the pain within my soul,
Helping me fill empty hole?
Shall I ever constant long
Holy places to belong?

119—Mem

The flavor of your Word,
    its sweetness
    like honey,

    comes not through the ears,
        my hearing
        and list'ning,

        nor only my feet,
            my actions
            my choices,

But your Word is with me,
    in my thoughts
    on my mind,

    giving me knowledge,
        and wisdom
        and insight,

D. P. Myers

    guiding my pathways,
        from evil
          to your truth.

I'm not just a hearer,
  but doer
  and lover,

  of your rules and laws,
    all day long
    all night long;

    thus, sweet is your Word
      to my heart
      forever.

119—Nun

A lighted path you've given me
That leads unto eternity.
Yet even though I walk in light
And in your ways I do delight,
Often darkness takes my soul
Exacting deep and painful toll.
Depressed and wanting long to hide
From lighted path my weak will guides,
Into the snares of wicked foe
My darkened feet will swiftly go,
And for a moment there is peace
Until I see there's no release
From present sin and wrath to come
Or from the one I have become.
Then in the darkness soft I hear
Sweet sounds and echoes that are dear—
The joyous sounds of your sweet Word
And promises from you I've heard.

A New Song

From my sin in which I wallow,
Light of yours again I follow,
Returning ever to the path
That leads to joy and not to wrath.
Lord, help me to in future days
My feet hold firm to lighted ways,
And in your Word much joy to find,
My heart to you ever inclined.

119—Samekh

I love your law,
    but I sometimes stray
        and walk pathways so dark.

I love your law,
    but my heart is pulled away
        down cold and haunting roads.

I look for warmth,
    a place to call home
        in the refuge of sinful places.

If only—

If only I were to love your law,
    A home I would find,
        a path would be lit,
            my feet would not stumble.

Do I not love your law?

D. P. Myers

119—Ayin

When darkness covers o'er the land
And seems like you have staid your hand,
When pain and loneliness oppress
And my life has become a mess,
Teach me to trust in all your ways,
Patiently living through each day.

When cause of pain I do not know
And long I wait for you to show,
When others tell me why you act
Yet lacking your omniscient fact,
Teach me your guiding hand to trust
And my impatience please adjust.

When heart breaks under painful tide
And questions bubble up inside,
When waves of fears near overtake
And I lie nightly long awake,
Teach me to trust your hidden love,
Your mercy raining from above.

Teach me to every false way hate
And while in pain on you to wait.
Above all teach me, Lord, to hold
Your words and ways higher than gold,
So when at last my course is run
I'll wake to hear you say, "Well done."

A New Song

119—Pe

Long my feet have daily tread
    Dark paths I've walked before.
Long this path has often led
    To darkened storms and more.

There are times my choices bear
    Fruit sour to the tongue.
There are times you drawn me near
    And sin from me you've wrung.

Some dear friends still hold me close,
    Full knowing who I am,
Yet to others I am gross,
    And by them I am damned.

In those moments when I've gone
    From fellowship so good,
For your face and word I long
    As hungry man for food.

In such dark and lonely days
    With heart's grief brimming full,
Thinking hard upon my ways,
    I long for a new soul.

Yet to me has not appeared
    A fresh breath blown within,
Stagnant then I live in fear
    Of full revealed sin.

Shout I fear that's loud and clear
    From towers tall and strong,
Shout for all the earth to hear
    All of the ways I'm wrong.

D. P. Myers

Fear that to the darkness then
    My feet will slowly go,
Even though I wait for when
    Your light will brightly glow.

Showing me a lighted path,
    A way for broken feet
From the shadows of your wrath
    Then to my Savior sweet.

Now I long for such a time
    Yet wander in a daze
Till I see your love sublime
    That lightens up my ways.

119—Tsade

Infinite beauty
    through holy words—
Infinite delight
    in holy God—

Finite sight
    through darkened eyes—
Finite joys
    in grimy man—

Small and despised
    among all sons—
Grand and glorious
    into the fray—

119—Qoph

You have founded them forever
    continually supported,
        with no beginning,
           in eternity,
              temporally echoing.

119—Resh

Through pain one day my life will bloom
    Into promised flower,
A garland for the great bridegroom
    In the wedding hour.

But till that time some thistles grow,
    Weeds ever crowding life.
And even though I better know,
    I'm often filled with strife.

Yet it is true I love your law,
    New life given through it.
This struggle is my fatal flaw
    'Tween weeds and life I sit.

Though ev'ry day some weeds I plant,
    Your ways I truly love.
So do for me those things I can't
    With your hand from above.

And guide a plow that tills the weeds
    And rips them from life's path.
For mercy's love is what I need
    To keep me from your wrath.

D. P. Myers

For in the end I know it's true
    The only way I live
Is loving all the words from you
    And Word in flesh you give.

119—Sin and Shin

The treasures of my heart are dung
    Compared to holy writ,
And from my soul dark dross is wrung
    When near to him I sit.

Yet still I long to taste the dirt
    Instead of God's sweet food,
And those around me do I hurt
    When in this deep dark mood.

But even so I want the law
    That comes from mouth of God,
And try to bow in holy awe,
    Forgetting paths I've trod.

Forget the paths of darkened past.
    Forget the longings deep.
I need from him a new heart cast
    And truth in me to seep.

So daily must I go to him
    And daily I must pray,
For in my heart is darkest sin
    That his love takes away.

A New Song

119—Taw

I seek the truth and who it's from
    For hours of the day,
But contradiction I've become,
    Pulled in many ways.

I long for face above to see,
    Guiding all my paths.
But oft' I only look in me,
    And hold to sinful wrath.

I long for holy hands to save
    Me from darkened road.
I long for holy blood that gave
    Me freedom from sin's goad.

But also found so deep within
    My affection seat,
A longing to run far again
    And actions to repeat.

Actions spring from dark desire.
    Thoughts give birth to words.
Words then set my heart on fire,
    And choices burn absurd.

Yet in this maelstrom of life,
    Still I love his law,
And though my heart is filled with strife,
    I look to him with awe.

Lord, save me from the ways I love,
    Deepest darkest joy,
And from my life all sin please shove
    And in its place employ

D. P. Myers

>Your hope and grace that deep I need,
>Your words and ways my heart to feed,
>So love can overcome my greed
>For sinful ways, O Lord, I plead.

120

Too long have I deceived
    Myself and those I know,
Too long have I received
    False praise from men below.

Now I find I tire
    Of stark duplicity,
Soon I will retire
    From what is false in me.

There's a constant battle,
    A war inside I fight,
Ever-constant prattle
    Of darkness to the light.

How to silence voices
    That live within my head—
Something that my choices
    Have to my failure led.

Tire of the voices,
    I know not what to do—
Tire of my choices
    That lead away from you.

Longing for a home built
    With God and friends so dear,
Sitting with intense guilt
    Has silenced such a cheer.

A New Song

Now it's time in my life,
    Like ev'ry single man,
When peace must conquer strife
    And open to God's plan.

Purge from me my dark heart,
    Take sin and guilt's dark smear.
Grant to me a new start
    With you and friends so dear.

121

You keep me, Lord, and hold my hand
    In those times when I stray.
You keep me safe within your land
    When my heart runs away.

I always need help from on high,
    I look to nature's strength.
I hold its beauty in my eye
    And search cross earth's full length.

But mountains hold no aid for me,
    Nor nature's lovely ways,
For only at your throne can be
    The help for my dark days.

122

Can ever some true joy
Come through a human ploy?
Will not our hearts cry out
And twist and scream and shout
When joys that we did take

D. P. Myers

Are found to be a fake?
It's in that darkest night
When joy is out of sight,
We often hear a call,
Slight echoes ever small.

This sound we hear is sweet
It calls to us to meet.
So through the night we run
To hope of dawn's new sun
With rays over the earth
Of light and joy and mirth
That shakes the darkest caves
And empties all the graves,
So death that was within
No longer found therein.

Joy's call continues long,
Loud grows this distant song.
This song from high above
Earth's lone song sung of love
That calls us to be free
From who we used to be.
It calls us to rejoice
With new and loud clear voice.
It calls us from our fears
And wipes away our tears.

The song draws ever near
Its words then do we hear,
"Come to the holy throne
And you'll not be alone.
All those who come are mine,
And I am ever thine.
You've looked for joy below,
But here you'll ever know
True joy and inner peace
That will not ever cease."

123

Mercy oft I long from you,
Yet I frequent evil do.

Evil heart is deep within,
It's the cause of all my sin.

Eyes I lift to heaven high,
Holy throne above the sky,

But in dark on earth I stay
Hiding from the holy ray.

Ray of light from holy heights
Wanting to shed mercy's light,

But I long in shadows stand,
Shame that keeps me from his land

Pushed me far from holy crown,
Hands of shame still drag me down

To a low and scornful place
Where in shame I hide my face.

Yet I hear in dark and cold
Soothing whisper ever bold,

"Won't you come to seek my face?
Won't you come to holy place?

Step from under shadow's fall,
Reach for me and hear my call,

Won't you come to see the Son?
Won't you turn from shameful run?"

D. P. Myers

Long I've run from mercy full
To a dark and hellish hole,

Yet he's tracked me where I roam,
Calling me to now come home.

124

How rarely do I struggle with
    Hard battles from without.
My darkened foes war in my pith,
    A long internal bout.

They scream and rage within my soul,
    They tear my heart in two.
So often this war takes its toll
    I know not what to do.

But then I see a hand that moves
    So slightly in the ranks,
It quells the soldiers in my shoes
    For respite I him thank.

The Lord who constant covers me
    Like snow from winter's night,
He hides the mess I often see
    Made from my inner fight.

In moments of my deep despair,
    Such respite do I love—
To know the name that lingers there
    And holds me from above.

A New Song

He holds me next to sacred side,
    He keeps me from the flood
Of sin and guilt that me betide
    And stains the white with mud.

But from his side there poureth true,
    From scar I scarce can see,
From ragged flesh there poureth through
    Blood washing over me.

It washes out the darkest stains.
    It wipes away the dirt.
And like the future fresh spring rain,
    It clears away my hurt.

Yet even now with battle fresh,
    And minions in my soul,
It's hard to trust and catch my breath
    Under the battle's toll.

125

Throughout my life my land has seen
    Dark foes on every side,
And through my life my heart has been
    Filled full with evil pride.

But only short will you allow
    Those forces in the land
Who uproot what the righteous plow
    With steady faithful hand.

You keep my soul protected from
    Such wicked evil ways.
Down from the mountains you have come
    To give eternal days.

D. P. Myers

You promise to the righteous man
    A respite from the fight,
And in your holy loving plan
    You banish dark with light.

So keep my soul now free from all
    Dark enemies within,
And take me to your holy hall
    Where I am free from sin.

126

From lands afar you brought
    The sons you took away,
And for their lives you fought
    Through years and in each day.
From prisons they have come,
    The exiles over seas,
And to your home they run
    To find their place with thee.

From chains that bound my soul
    With darkness evermore,
From deepest sin's dark hole,
    With love my soul you tore.
You tore me from my hell
    And brought me back to you,
Your work in me will tell
    Of all your blood can do.

But still there are more men
    Cast far in distant land
That often ask just when
    You'll free them with your hand.

A New Song

Each day with heavy chain
    They serve lords from afar.
Each day with sweat and pain
    They seek for where you are.

Yet even though I'm free
    By all that you have done
And even though I see
    That to you men will run,
There in my soul remains
    A love so dark and black
That fills my day with pains
    And heavy bends my back.

I want you to return
    To free the captive last,
And from my soul to burn
    My sin from future's past.
With joy then will I tread,
    With pleasure I will sing
Of life brought from the dead,
    To the presence of the King.

127

My life I often think I plan.
    My steps I take them strong.
But ways I chose I frequent ran
    And found them ever wrong.

My labor had produced in me
    Nights worry on my bed
Until my eyes at last did see
    That by you I am led.

D. P. Myers

Unless I place my hand in thine
    And trust in your right ways,
I'll never see your glory shine
    With blessings in dark days.

128

You promise blessings from above
    In life lived here below.
You promise happiness and love
    To those who love you so.
Tables filled with food and drink,
    And wife will fertile be.
The children at my table drink
    Of wine that comes from thee.
The city that I live within
    Is guided by your hand,
And children's children ever win
    A peace upon the land.

But here I sit in middle age
    With finger ringless still,
And ever as I turn life's page
    I find I have no will—
No will to seek for earthly bride
    To walk along life's way
And stem the lonely empty tide
    That washes through each day.
No children's children have I near,
    My tribe has pushed me far,
And all that once I held so dear
    Has left my heart with scars.

I thought my feet had walked your paths,
    I thought I loved you so,

A New Song

But life of mine deserves your wrath,
    For down dark paths I go.
My empty hand and empty heart
    Comes not from fear of you
But from my paths that oft' depart
    From lighted paths so true.
Down paths so true where blessings lay
    I wish my feet would tread,
I wish my heart would find its way
    From pathways of the dead.

129

From dusty ground a cloud comes forth,
    from feet constrained by chains,
        with backs broken by the work
            of evil men's dark will.
But never can they change the worth
    of men under their reign,
        never whip that flesh does jerk
            be ever free to kill.

These wicked men will ever be
    like grass in desert dry,
        growing quickly with the dew
            and burning in the sun.
And never in eternity
    will holy God's mouth cry,
        "Blessings ever over you
            and to my courts now run."

But all dark foes that scar my back
    are not from lands afar,
        oft' they come from lusts within
            that tear my soul in two.

D. P. Myers

They war and rage and oft' attack
    my will, and then they scar
        heart and then deep ruts of sin
            long keeps my life from you.

These foes so dark that live in me
    shall never prosper long.
        Son shall rise and conquer them
            and burn them from my life.
And someday soon will I be free
    to sing a vict'ry song
        and see holy diadem
            that conquered all my strife.

130

Darkest night with colors gone,
    Soul's dark ache and muted song.
Endless pit and shadows gloom,
    Hellish soul in darkened room.
Watchman waits for break of day.
    From the depths you hear me say,
"When will your light this way come?
    When will your grace have I some?"

The blackest night slowly breaks,
    This heart of mine lesser aches.
Through cloudy sky peeks the sun,
    From heart and soul darkness runs.
Muted shades now bright with rays,
    Soul delights in holy ways.
All that once was colored dull
    Shines with love from holy hall.

A New Song

Scintillating colors new,
    Tearful eyes wiped dry by you.
Darkest shades outlined by light,
    Brightest day conquers the night.
Basking face in sunny glow,
    Mercy for my sins you show.
Hope eternal held in thee,
    Strongest chains broken for me.

Yet day's dusk returns again,
    Darkest pit filled deep with sin.
Shadows conquer colored fields,
    Will of mine to evil yields.
Fading light at days dark end,
    In the pit my soul I send.
Darkest night with colors gone,
    Souls dark ache and muted song.

131

How hard it is to calm one's soul
    When storm clouds settle in,
And when in life there grows a hole
    Where dark storms rage within.

But often holes are dug by choice
    And built by reaching hands
That claw and scrape to find a voice
    To sing of foreign lands—

Of lands afar I'll never tread
    And paths I'll never see.
Such longing builds within me dread
    Until I rest in thee.

D. P. Myers

Lord, when in you I find my hope,
    And when in you I rest,
Your peace enables me to cope
    Like birds within a nest.

132

Your servant son has built a house
    For holy God to dwell.
Your servants place the beam and stone
    And 'cross the land we tell—

We tell of refuge from the storms,
    Of famine and decay.
We tell of holy sacred forms,
    Of love and joy someday.

Yet in this day of grimy life
    Our hands plunge in life's mud,
Though in that day of broken strife
    We're cleansed by crimson flood.

133

Far up north the mountain stands
Tow'ring over verdant lands.
Roots run deep, and peaks stand high,
Snowcapped triplets in the sky.
Winter snows and summer rays
Water lands through heat-filled days.
Fruit and grain for all to eat
Owes its life to snow's high seat.

A New Song

Brothers down time's path they go,
Wisdom they to each do show.
Treasures hidden deep within,
Talents of their closest kin.
Brothers walk through troubled times
But in unity they climb
Pathways cluttered oft' with strife
Leading to a pleasant life.

Far above the earth below
Sits transcendent holy stow
Waiting for God's holy plan—
Blessings poured out onto man.
Onto those who love his law,
Onto those through hope who saw
One who came from heaven's store,
One who gives life evermore.

134

When bright dawn breaks across the land,
    Devout men raise holy hands.
When pleasant times in life are seen,
    Joy lights up a happy mien.
But holy God must still be blessed
    When dark times keep us from rest.
When dim dusk falls and lights go out,
    When souls in pain scream and shout,
It's still the time to bless the one
    Who made all and sent his Son.

D. P. Myers

135

Power from our God on high—
Verdant earth and azure sky,
Lightning strikes and thunder rolls,
Gusty winds wreak earthly tolls.

Hand of God has paved the way,
Blessèd work and joyful day,
Striking foes and crushing down,
Claiming souls for his renown.

Mind of man on earth below,
Crafty hands and talents grow,
Forming earth and storing hoard,
Idols take eyes from the Lord.

Men of earth lift up your hands,
Families to holy lands.
Look up high and praise our God,
Joyful paths for men of sod.

Voices high we lift to him,
Feeble hearts with dirty sin.
Idols draw and divert sight
Even as we know what's right.

Lord, we want to worship you,
Make our broken hearts anew.
Take us from the idol's pull,
Clean the pathways of our soul.

A New Song

136

Why does my praise so hardly flow
When hand of God doeth clearly go
Through earth and sky and universe
And even to my little verse?

Why ever do my eyes not see
The ways his love provides for me,
The way he works through all that is
To make of me a son of his?

Why ever is my soul downcast
When love of his eternal lasts,
When steadfast is his loving hand
That brings me to a holy land?

When ever will my heart leap high
To see his hand throughout the sky,
To see his hand in earth below,
Lord, will my heart such sights not know?

When will I know his love so pure
Or sense his steady hand so sure?
Will full I ever bend my knee
So one day I'll his glory see?

137

Days of joy and glory fade
    Far down the halls of time—
For much goodness we were made
    And future days of thine.

D. P. Myers

But we sit with captor foe
    By darkened waters far—
Aching hearts now long to know
    Bright city's morning star.

Holy city on a hill
    With safe tall walls so strong,
Toward it have I bent my will
    And deepest heart does long.

But my painful days I live
    In chains with song that's mute,
And my mem'ries often give
    A vengeance resolute.

Judgment wished upon the head
    Of foes with evil new—
Holy, painful, awful dread
    For those who reject you.

But the enemies I meet,
    They pale in compare
To he who stands upon my feet
    And from the mirror stares.

Deep within this heart of mine
    A wicked vein does run,
Spoiling holy goodness thine
    And blotting out your Son.

Darkness haunts my ev'ry verse,
    It spoils ev'ry note.
I hope love will soon reverse
    My ever-silent throat.

Lead me then to city pure,
    Forgive my sinful ways.
Pave for me a path that's sure
    And straight for all my days.

A New Song

138

Pain through which I present tread
Ends in fields of the dead.

All men surely walk this path—
Streets of trouble, streets of wrath.

Treading down life's path can be
With the Lord or only me.

Lonely steps and empty days,
Somber face and darkened ways.

Steady through these times your hand
Leads the lowly through the land.

Troubles come, and troubles go,
But I through it all still know

Even in the midst of pain,
Deepest loss is for my gain—

Paths of trouble often bring
Wisdom for my lips to sing

Praises to the God on high
Sung until the day I die.

Yet behind each joyful song
Broken hearts still deeply long

For ways free from wicked man
And his ever-harmful plan.

Strength I need to live this life
In the face of constant strife,

D. P. Myers

For life ends not in the grave
But on streets with gold you pave.

139

My feet walk down the paths I choose,
    And words fall from my tongue.
But words and ways and all I use
    All from God's will are wrung.

My darkest steps and brightest days
    Are ever under him,
And even when far are my ways,
    I hang from holy limb.

My life is fruit on branch divine
    My steps known far before,
Before there was a pregnant sign
    God had my days in store.

Yet even so doth anger rage
    When wicked men run free,
When sins and darkness from this age
    Corrupt all I can see.

And in this life of holy writ,
    I still free choose my path.
Such knowledge wonderful is it,
    Yet still deserve I wrath.

Lord, purge my heart of sinful thoughts.
    Wipe clean my slate of sin.
So flee from you my feet do not,
    And plans of yours do win.

A New Song

140

The traps I find along life's path
Are spread for me by men of wrath.
They're hidden under leaf of tree
Near fruited bush for all to see,
Near wicked men in deep disguise
Who hides the evil from my eyes.
For fruited bush my heart so longs,
It writes the words of my life songs.
But hand to bush and fruit to tongue
Finds feet entrapped and mouth in dung.
The wicked men then drop their mask
And with a laugh they raise a cask
And drink so deep on mortal sin
That from the fruit now lies within.
Within my life the juices flow,
They numb my heart so I don't know
The right from wrong on earth below.

When knowledge of the good departs
There is no guilt within my heart.
These wicked men beside the way
My eyes catch glimpse and then I say,
"You aren't the men I thought I knew."
"Oh, yes," they say, "for we are you.
You are the man who lays the trap
For you to leave the righteous map—
The map that shows you how to live,
The map your Lord died to you give,
The map your open eyes once saw,
Showing the traps defined by law.
But days of past you threw it out
And happily with lusty shout
Declared that you no longer need
The hands on cross that crimson bleed,
The hands that transform sinful seed.

D. P. Myers

So now as fruit from bush you take,
A blackened heart you fin'lly make
To pump through veins a sinful juice,
And now your moral bounds are loose."
My face I see reflected there
And know my evil eyes do stare
Back from the mask of wicked man,
The one who seeks to thwart God's plan,
His plan that always seeks my good
And satisfies with holy food.
"Your holy food, Lord, let me find
And banish from me wicked rind,
The rind my evil self did eat
When from your path wandered my feet.
Over my heart let justice roll,
Extract me from the darkest hole,
And by your blood redeem my soul."

141

How easy life can be
    When the gap is plain to see
    Between men of ill intent
And others heaven-sent.

How clear my prayers are
    To heaven's bright throne afar
    For protection from such men
Who lure to sinful den.

But life is not so clear
    When the evil men are dear,
    When the light and dark don't part
In friends' and my own heart.

A New Song

The days are dark and bleak
    When the wicked men will seek
    To destroy good servant's life
And trample down with strife.

Yet harm I don't refuse
    From the servants you would choose,
    From the servants who would cleanse
And make us holy men.

Lord, keep me from sin's harm
    And protect me with your arm.
    Lord, protect my battered soul
And love will make me whole.

142

Deep within my heart there lies
Scars and pains and mournful cries—
    Scars from hurtful men around,
    Pains from tumbling to the ground,
    Cries from both a wrenching sound.

All along my path so clear
Are the traps of sin I fear—
    Traps laid down by wicked men,
    Sinful paths to where I've been,
    Fearful dark and evil den.

Even with temptation strong,
Still for helping hands I long—
    Hands that take me from old path,
    Hands that keep me from your wrath,
    Hands that wash in crimson bath.

D. P. Myers

Earthly hands are what I know.
I need hands not here below—
    Hands that will redeem my life,
    Hands to clear away my strife,
    Hands to cut with holy knife.

Cut me deep to clear my name.
Cut away my sin and shame.
    Take from me my shame so deep.
    Give me righteous tears to weep.
    Cut a new path to God's keep.

143

Down at lonely table
    far into the night,
I know I am able
    to fly so far from light.

So quickly do I fly
    far away from good
Into dark evil sky
    to seek for deadly food.

But even as I soar
    far away from you,
Your mercy's loving roar
    calls to my soul, "Renew!"

But as my flight turns back
    to the golden sun,
The sky with minions black
    hinders my homeward run.

A New Song

Your mercies lift my wings
    high above the fray.
Your voice forgiveness sings
    and calls me unto day,

And to a future feast
    with your holy fare
Where greatest to the least
    dine with the Godhead there.

144

Breath of God, life of man,
    breathing in, breathing out...
Shadows pass, none can stand,
    shadows low, going out...

Lord holds back enemies,
    breathing in, breathing out...
Lord calms dark stormy seas,
    shadows low, going out...

Man is blessed with good life,
    breathing in, breathing out...
Fortress from war and strife,
    shadows low, going out...

    But oft I find
    That life can grind
    Even those of holy mind.

    And oft I see
    Evil can be
    Firmly planted like a tree.

D. P. Myers

    And long it lives
    And often gives
    Painful days to men of his.

    So why do I
    Seek holy eye
    To shine blessings from on high

    If breath and light
    And shadows plight
    Is the length of earthly flight?

Blessed of God, simple son,
    breathing in, breathing out...
To your lap do I run,
    shadows low, going out...

Held so tight, holy arms,
    breathing in, breathing out...
Keep me safe from all harms,
    shadows low, going out...

Words anew, through the land,
    breathing in, breathing out...
Shadows fly, life's short span,
    shadows low, now gone out.

145

Voices many sing your praise,
To the Lord our song we raise.

Brook and field, rock and tree,
In creation do we see
Hand of God and glory bright,
Works of wisdom in plain sight.

A New Song

Love and mercy for all man
Amply offered in God's plan,
Calling out through darkest plight,
Man forgiven in your sight.

Unto you our voices sing,
To your throne our lives we bring.

146

Faithful is the Lord of all
Even to those of the fall.
Food and shelter does he give,
Freedom's light for all to live.
Faithful is the God on high,
For our sins he came to die,
Lifting up those stooped so low,
Love eternal here to know.

But instead I oft' trust man,
Taking comfort where I can,
Longing for a faithful touch,
Longing to be loved through much,
Seeking for a constant friend,
One to whom my heart can bend,
One for me whose love is true,
Near to me in old and new.

But such friends can never be
A true friend to set me free,
Free from sin and darkest night,
Free from life's bleak evil plight.
True hope cometh from above,
From hands stained by crimson love.
Praises then on high I lift
For your love's eternal gift.

D. P. Myers

147

Beauties from your hand abound,
Nature's joys are all around—
Mountains tall and valleys low,
Both you blanket in white snow.
Brooks and stream then river strong
Filled with rain from cloudy throng.
Fruit and harvest both depend
On rain found at river's end.

Hands reach low to lift up high
Those who weep with tearful eye—
Poor of heart and trodden down,
Cleaned and clothed with loving gown.
Wicked men you've cast away,
Banished from eternal day.
Laws of yours and Son of man
Sent to us through chosen clan.

Praise for all your works we give!
Praise for all that helps us live!
Praise for beauty in the land!
Praise for mercy from your hand!
But of works on land and sea,
There's but one that pleases thee—
Heart of man who fears the Lord
Living life by sacred Word.

A New Song

148

In the ground the blocks you place
    That brings forth leaf and tree.
From the dirt, and by your grace
    You make all that we see.

Hill and peak and bird and beast,
    The sea's deep creatures all,
From the greatest to the least,
    Your praise their voices call.

Then from dirt the man you wrought
    In image of yours fair.
From our mouths your praise is brought
    In thanks for loving care.

Thanks we give for all you've done,
    Your works sing praises loud.
Plant and fowl and fish and son,
    Unto your throne have bowed.

But of the works, all that you do,
    The one that is the best—
Your only Son sent from you
    Who brings us all to rest.

Praises from the heavens high
    And praise from earth below.
To your throne beyond the sky,
    All praise to you will go.

D. P. Myers

149

Voices high your praise we sing,
Honor glory to the king.
Tongue and lip formed for your joy,
All for you do we employ.
In your courts and on our beds,
Praise and song for you have led
Saints in battle over foes,
You have conquered all our woes.

But can those who sing to you
Raise high sword and wicked hew?
And voice raised up to the sky,
Can it utter battle cries?
Can your sons of holy peace
Become tools of evil's ccase?
Become weapons you employ
To kill evil and bring joy?

Lord, our praise we bring to thee
At your throne with bended knee.
Humbly waiting on your call,
You we honor with our all.
Yet with all your ways unknown
I pray mercy to be shown
For those men of wicked soul
Once was me whom you've made whole.

A New Song

150

So full of myst'ry are your ways—
You guide our paths and plan our days.
You sit on throne above the sky,
Yet to this earth you came to die.

Our praise to you we offer free—
Our dance, our song, our bended knee.
With voices loud and trumpet clear,
Our praise to you comes forth from cheer.

Yet also do we sing when low,
And in our sadness still we show
That praise to you our voices guide
In times when we've been tossed aside.

And those times when we don't feel
That our souls your love will heal—
Yes, in those days when there's no thrill,
Our tongues will praise you even still.

Lord, teach us how to sing to you
And praise your mercies ever new—
Your mercies seen at dawn's first light,
Your mercies helping us through night.

Our Lord, we praise and you adore
For us you've opened heaven's store
And poured upon us mercies all,
So to your throne our praises call.

Chapter 4
Creative Ways to Respond to God's Word

Now that you've read through the poems or most likely have at least perused some of them, it may be helpful if I explain some of the influences behind the creation of some of these new songs. The first thing to state is that each poem was written as a response to reading the Word. They did not come as a result of me living and thinking in a vacuum. In his book *Life as Worship*, John Kitchen says, "Worship is made up of the intricate, rhythmic weaving of revelation and response. God speaks. We respond." Our worship is a response to God's words. And while I don't wish to discount worship as a result of God's work in nature, I would suggest that truly focused worship comes as a result of encountering his daily accessible words in Scripture (though discussing such a distinction is not the scope of this present work).

The starting point for each poem was the reading of Scripture followed by prayer and meditation on the text. Then during this time of meditation and prayer, images and thoughts would lead me to composing the first line of the poem, which was often the most difficult portion of the poem. After the first image was in my mind and the first line on the page, I often sat at my desk in prayer and meditation for a few additional hours before the poem was completed and in its first rough form. Months following the completion of the last poem, I then took more time and a couple of drafts to edit each poem into a more presentable form.[7] It was during the editing that I catalogued some of the approaches (listed in the following sections) used in writing the poems. While this list is certainly not exhaustive, I hope it may be helpful to you as you read and worshipfully respond to the work of the Word and the Spirit in your life.

Construct of the Text

One of the first things I do when reading a passage of Scripture is to spend time to understand the structure and the outline of the text. I've found that when I understand a text's structure, I gain additional insights that were not available upon first glance. However, I won't go so far as to say that the meaning is in the structure, but the structure certainly offers insight beyond the mere words themselves. By way of example, when reading the book of Genesis, I found that it is helpful to know that the phrase "of the generations" (*towledah* in Hebrew) partitions the book into ten major sections. Each section tracks the progress of God's hand through history from Adam to Jacob. Thus, by being aware of the repetition of this phrase, I am able to understand the basic outline of Genesis, from which I can then begin to process the meaning of the included narratives.

Yet for some reason in the past when I've read the Psalms, I rarely analyzed the structure. I think this was because I saw them as poetry and thus not entirely rational in their construct—an assumption that I've found to be horribly misguided. I have found that each psalm has an outline by which we can understand its content, and furthermore, there is often a greater structure organizing the placement of each psalm in its place in each of the five books as well as the larger book of the Psalms. One of the structures of particular interest to me during this process was

---

[7] I struggled with the tension between keeping the rough and raw poems intact or polishing them so that they would be of higher quality as measured by human standards. But after deciding to present these poems to a wider audience, I chose to err on the side of polishing them so their rhyme, meter, and flow would have a more aesthetic appeal. If this somehow detracts from the integrity of the book, I apologize. I trust you will accept this *edited* book of poetry.

the acrostic. I found that nine psalms were written as an acrostic where each verse begins with the successive letters of the Hebrew alphabet.[8] But of them all, it was Psalm 37 to which my attention was most drawn.

After a first reading, it seemed that there was a structure under the surface, but I couldn't put my finger on it, so I began to write a summary statement of each verse. What seemed to emerge were three major themes structured in a fairly tight outline with introductions and transitions. But after consulting numerous commentaries and scholarly works I nearly discarded my outline because the majority of these scholars saw Psalm 37 merely as a random collection of proverbial sayings. Additionally, many of these scholars went so far as to label the acrostic form in the Psalms as lowbrow poetry. They claimed that the psalmists sacrificed content for the artificial poetic structure of an acrostic. However, being stubborn as I am, these claims did not set well with me.

I was convinced that there was something to the structure and a depth in Psalm 37 that others may have missed. I realize that this sounds arrogant to say that I've seen something that scholars have not, but the evidence seemed overwhelming. While I had to grant the possibility that I might be reading into Scripture my thoughts (eisegesis) and not pulling out of Scripture God's thoughts (exegesis) I continued to study Psalm 37. I spent more time outlining it, labeling each section with the appropriate Hebrew letter, rewriting it in my own words, and finally writing summary statements. I even made a trip to see a professor from seminary to ask him about his opinion on the subject. And while he didn't say definitively that my thoughts were correct, he admitted that my basic thoughts were most likely heading down the right path and that it's certainly possible that the published scholars had missed something.

Encouraged by his words and after some further work, I concluded that Psalm 37 had three main themes within it, namely (1) the demise of wicked men, (2) the promise of an inheritance, and (3) a call to

---

[8] Five chapters in Book One of the Psalms (9, 10, 25, 34, 37) and four in Book Five (111, 112, 119, 145) are written in an acrostic form. Not every acrostic psalm is complete, as some are missing letters and some have letters placed in an improper order. Of all the acrostics, Psalm 37 and Psalm 119 are the only two that appear to be complete in their current form, although there is some debate concerning Psalm 37's completeness. For further study in this area, see the works by Freedman and Maloney listed in the bibliography.

righteousness. Furthermore, these themes didn't appear to be randomly strewn throughout the psalm as many scholars claimed, but they were found in an order that one might encounter in a well-formed sermon. The psalm begins by introducing the three main themes (vv. 1–6). The main body of the sermon is then sectioned into three parts, the first of which discusses the way of the evil men (vv. 7–20), the second the promise of a righteous inheritance (vv. 21–29), and the third a call to righteous living (vv. 30–33). It then concludes with a short summary of the three main points (vv. 34) before restating these themes in verses 35–36 (way of the evil man), 37–38 (an inheritance), and 39–40 (a call to righteousness). While there are some minor exceptions to this structure (which bear further study), I am convinced that Psalm 37 is not a collection of random proverbial statements. Such a view doesn't seem to do justice to the intent of the psalmist or to the content of the psalm. My study of Psalm 37, which took a few weeks, helped to organize my thoughts and prepare my response. I wanted to retain something of the structure and content in my poem but still make my response a personal and genuine one. Thus, I settled on a structure that begins with an introduction of the three themes followed by sections developing each theme and concluding with a restatement of the themes again.

Scripture's Vivid Imagery

The Scripture's vivid imagery, which is used in many psalms to convey what is on the author's heart, also became a source for my own imagination. The first instance of this is Psalm 1:3, where David likens the righteous man to a tree as he says,

> He is like a tree
> > planted by streams of water
> that yields its fruit in season,
> > and its leaf does not wither.

As I read these words, I was reminded that many other trees appear elsewhere in Scripture. The first that came to mind were the two trees in the garden of Eden—the Tree of Knowledge of Good and Evil and the Tree of Life. From the garden where these two trees were planted flowed four rivers that watered the land. I wondered about the relationship between the trees and the life-giving water that flowed to the plants and animals in the garden, and it was not long before I thought of another tree from which a life-giving flow poured. In the Gospels, a hewn tree was used as a cross, upon which Christ, the Word become flesh, hung. And flowing down this tree was a stream of Christ's life-giving blood, granting eternal life to all who would receive it. But these weren't the only trees standing near a life-giving flow. In Revelation 22, there stands another tree spanning the river flowing from God's throne in the middle of the New Jerusalem—the Tree of Life. Its fruit and its leaves are used for the healing of the nations.

As I thought about each of these trees, I wondered if they might in some way be intimately related to the liquid that flows nearby. And furthermore, I wondered if there was any connection between these trees. Thus, the poem resulting from Psalm 1 starts with the images of trees found in Scripture and continues into an imaginative interpretation. This is something that I've also done throughout this collection with other images the psalmists used that describe God as a fortress, that speak of paths lighted by his Word, that tell of our own pits of darkness and despair, and that outline many other images. The Psalms often use poetic images, and so it seemed right that poetic responses would do likewise.

Placing Myself in the Psalmist's Shoes

While structure and images were powerful and frequent catalysts for the poems in this volume, they certainly weren't the only influences precipitating a poetic response. Many poems were written as a response to me asking if I could say the same thing the psalmist said. For instance, in Psalm 23, the psalmist says, "The Lord is my shepherd, I shall not want." But I wondered if it was accurate for me to say that he truly is *my* shepherd. I mean I *know* that he is, but do I *see* him as my shepherd and do I *act* as though he is? Furthermore, am I satisfied enough with him so that I want for nothing more than him? Do I rest in him, knowing that he shepherds me through the troubles, trials, and pains of life, or do I resort to worry? Do I know that the struggles of life can be endured because he is with me? Do I trust in him, or do I seek other means of getting through the trials of life?

Psalm 23 continues and says, "Even though I walk through the valley of the shadow of death, I will fear no evil for you are with me." Do I fully realize that when I walk through tough times that he is there, or do I revel in the feelings of loneliness? Do I realize that the psalmist doesn't say that God will take us from them but that he is *with us* in the midst of these trials? As such, am I ready to walk dark paths of trouble, rejection, and temptations, knowing he is there and not necessarily taking me from them? I know I long for deliverance and for my tears to be dried, but am I ready for God to allow me to suffer and even die, not having seen justice or deliverance? I realize that Christ taught us to pray that the Father would "deliver us from evil" (Matthew 6:13) and that he promises that he will "wipe every tear from our eye" (Revelation 21:4), but I also know that many of his followers died in torturous ways, "not having received what was promised" (Hebrews 11:39). It was with these and other questions in mind that I penned the poem for Psalm 23. I also used this same process of placing myself in the position of the author and asking myself numerous questions for many of the other poems in this volume.

Current Life Events

Current personal events and experiences also influenced many of these poems. For example, I was reading Psalm 112 during a week of difficult personal struggles that left me feeling empty, dry, blank, and unable to write anything in response. One morning after going to the Word and not knowing what to write, I put the Bible aside and read an article in which the author relied heavily on historical context as *the* key to unlocking the *true* meaning of a number of passages of Scripture. And even though he did proper historical work, I found that I didn't agree with his conclusions.

It was interesting to me that he and I had processed the same text and yet arrived at such drastically different interpretations. Unable to explain how he arrived at his conclusion, I began to think through how I drew my conclusions on the text in question.

I realized that for the most part when I approach the Scripture, I try to let it speak for itself, but I also rely on the scriptural and historical context to aid my understanding of the passage. Even though I might be vigilant in seeking to know what God is saying, I also know that it's impossible for me to keep my culture, personal beliefs, longings, and desires from influencing how I encounter the text. With this in mind, I looked back at the article and recognized that the author had kept most of those influences out of his approach. It appeared that he was genuinely seeking to be consistent with the text. But it also appeared that since he was leaning so heavily on the historical context as *the* interpreter of Scripture, he was also implying that unless we have access to history, then we will never grasp the Scripture's true meaning. But if this is true, then how I can know if I am viewing the proper and complete history? Maybe some historical facts have yet to be uncovered that will finally give the proper view. Furthermore, how can I keep my own personal history and biases out of the history I select and ultimately out of my interpretation of the text? Needless to say, I spent a fairly long time thinking through many questions like these regarding the influences on my reading of Scripture.

I spent so much time thinking about these questions that I felt as though I was running in a circle. Frustrated, I put the article down and reread Psalm 112, finding in the first verse these words, "Blessed is the man who fears the Lord, who greatly delights *in his commandments!*" While certainly not the final word (and maybe not even a partial word) on hermeneutic debates, I realized that the Word of God was sufficient for its own purposes. Now I don't mean to say that historical context is irrelevant, but it must be seen in its proper place, namely as an aid to uncover subtleties and nuances, not to change the *prima facie* reading of the text.⁹ It is when I read his Word—and only his Word—that I find delight in him and in his commandments. And with this in mind, I meditated on Psalm 112:1, questioning if I was truly delighting in his Word and learning to properly fear the Lord or if I was going to the Word with my own agenda, wearing a pair of biased glasses through which to see in Scripture meanings that would be pleasing to me regardless of their truth value. With such thoughts, my poem began as follows:

> Do I fear you Lord?
>   Do I love your Word?
> Will I change my life
>   To match what I've heard?

I realized that day that I had often missed the point of reading and meditating on Scripture. I was searching for some deep and transcendent truth that applies to all of humanity but had forgotten to ask the question about what God wanted of me and how he wanted to mold my life.

Even though we must not neglect proper study by utilizing every tool at our command, we must not forget that Scripture is like a two-edged sword piercing the soul and spirit and discerning the thoughts and intentions of the heart (Hebrews 4:12). We are also told that it is a mirror into which we look to see who we are and by which we realize who we must be (James 1:22–25). It's not only an historical document with wonderful structure, but it's also a living document through which God desires to do a radical work in our lives. As a result, many of my poems were the product of being cut in two by the sword of Scripture or contemplating my reflection in its mirror.

---

[9] This topic is, of course, of vital importance and certainly not settled in all areas of scholarly debate. In fact, many of the theological issues of the day hinge on this very point regarding the role of historical context in scriptural interpretation. It is not my intention summarily to dismiss such a valuable debate, but when reading Scripture for personal devotional purposes, I haven't found the historical context to be of *primary* importance.

D. P. Myers

Moments in Life

Finally, though certainly not exhaustively, there were times when experiences of the day influenced the poems. One morning, as I always do after breakfast, I was on a walk with my two Labrador Retrievers. The rays of sun were coming through the trees and speckling the freshly cut grassy field when the two dogs took off running. For a moment I was tempted to call them back, but they seemed content, even happy, so I held my peace and let them run. Even now as I write this explanation months later, I can see them with their ears flopping and tails wagging as they chased whatever it is that dogs find to chase. It was in that moment as they were running around the field that I felt a sense of peace and comfort as if all was right with the world. I don't mean to suggest that this was a deep and great spiritual revelation, but that brief moment allowed me to realize that God grants us pleasure even in the small and insignificant things of life.

When I returned from the walk and to my desk, I read Psalm 119:1–8 (Aleph). It says, "Blessed are those whose way is blameless, who walk in the law of the Lord!" Scripture says that people are blessed, and I have often wondered what that really means. I know that more often than not, it means that when we follow a deeply spiritual truth or path, God's blessing is soon to follow. But I also think sometimes his blessings come to us in more pedestrian ways—the dew on the grass, the sun across the ocean, the mist on the mountains, even the gentle flop of dog's ears as he romps across a field. All of these blessings, though available to everyone regardless of belief, can also be small blessings that God bestows upon his children in their moments of need. Thus, while not the loftiest spiritual image possible and certainly not the poem I would have chosen to use as the start of my responses to the great Psalm 119, my poem on Psalm 119:1–8 (Aleph) begins with the image of God's general blessing of a dog romping in a field. Such a blessing led me to a broader appreciation of how God's blessings flow from following his law and Word.

Chapter 5
Final Thoughts: A New Song

While the previous descriptions weren't the only influences during the writing of this volume of Psalms poetry, they are some of the more prominent ones. I trust they may give you an adequate glimpse into some of the many ways that poetic responses to the Psalms might be formed. Even more, I hope they may be of help as you consider responding to Scripture with your own creative voice. And while this volume is a poetic response to the Psalms, I would encourage you to consider how to worshipfully respond to other portions of Scripture. Most likely you are aware of songs, poems, and other works of art that have been produced as a result of interaction with the narratives of the Old Testament, the Gospels, the book of Acts, the book Revelation, the Prophets, and even the Epistles. In like manner we must realize that our worshipful responses should not be limited to the Psalms but can—and should—come from our prayerful interaction with the whole of Scripture.

This leads me to my final topic—why I titled this book *A New Song*. This was not a title that came to me quickly, and even now I'm uncertain if it's the best choice. After all, this is not a work where I have attempted to write new songs in my own words while retaining the original flow of each psalm, though that has happened in a number of instances. Rather, as you may know, if you have read through any of the poems, the psalms were a springboard or a starting point from which I engaged with God in the context of my own life. Admittedly, mine is a life spent in melancholy moods as I rarely sing, rarely shout for joy, and rarely act as the optimist.

Yet even so, as I read through the book of Psalms, I find a glimmer of hope that I might never see. In fact, it may be that my melancholy disposition is what drew me to the Psalms in the first place. In the Psalms I found authors laying out their heart to God, fully wanting and expecting to be heard but frequently asking why it seemed that they weren't. And while there are many psalms ringing with obvious praise, there are also many that dive into the muck and grime of a disappointing life.

And so as I sat back after editing the poems to consider titles for this collection, I was struck with the graciousness of God that he would be willing to listen to our cries for help. He doesn't seem to be annoyed at all by the pain we express in the face of life. In fact, the contrary seems to be true. He seems to encourage it. He is our Father, and we are like newborn babes who stretch and cry inconsolably, not fully knowing what it is that we want or need. We feel empty inside, and yet we know that he is the only one able to satisfy us, even though we know not how and we know not when. And so we cry. We wail. We groan in ways that betray our wants but not in a way that understands our need. We are quite literally crying in the dark.

But in these times of despair and in this life of blindness, he speaks to us. A small shaft of light pokes through the darkness, and we are drawn toward it, for we were made with eyes that desire light. This distant glimmering shaft of light often reveals to us—if sometimes only for a moment—the beauty and the danger of the world around us. It guides us and comforts us. And when, for whatever reason, we no longer see that light, we are left with its memory lingering in the dark and often permeating our soul. Its memory produces a new way of seeing the world and a new way of encountering the darkness. We know there's a way out, and we know there's more than what our darkened lives have encountered. And just as we know that the eye is made for light and for seeing, we also know that the heart is made for experiencing and singing. And so, there in the darkness, our heart sings. It sings of the memory of the light. It sings of the beauty we encountered in that brief moment when the light pierced the darkness. It sings of our longing. And yet its songs are never perfect, for they come forth from a heart that is broken.

I think God understood this when he inspired the psalmist's heart and pen. I think the psalmists understood this when they composed. And I think the editors and compilers of the Psalms understood this when they put the book together into its final form. They all knew that we sing in the darkness about the glimmer of light that God has enabled us to see. They know we sing in the hope that one day the darkness will break away, revealing the full glory of God. And they know we sing because our heart's language is song, and it is through song that we were designed to approach our Savior.

And so just as God waited to see what Adam would name the animals, I think he also waits to hear our new songs. He waits to hear these new songs formed through our experiences—both good and bad—that will be unique to each of us. He knows that they will come as a result of God's faithfulness and love in our lives (Psalm 33). They will come as a result of his deliverance from the pits in our lives (Psalm 40). They will come as a result of the salvation he gives and the work he has done (Psalm 96). They will come as a result of his glorious work in nature (Psalm 98). They will come as a result of his promise to rescue us from those who seek our harm (Psalm 144). And they will come as a result of being part of the throng of God's servants he has empowered to fight for justice (Psalm 149).

And so I chose to call this collection of poems *A New Song*, as they are some of my new songs to God. I'm certain that they aren't the poems others would have written, but they're mine. I'm also certain that they're not the poems I'd write now if I were to repeat this process. For just as life's path and patterns change, so also would the poem's meter, rhyme, and content. We win some old battles, and we engage new ones. We fail where we once succeeded, and we succeed where we once failed. We mature in some areas, and in others we find that we have regressed. Our lives are dynamic and changing. But through it all, the various glimpses of light we are allowed to see do not change. And so we sing songs that are about both the unchanging light as well as the ever-tumultuous darkness of our lives into which the light shines.

I trust that you will find these poems to be an encouragement to you in your daily walk with Christ. I trust that you will find them to be catalysts for you as you consider how you can respond worshipfully to God's Word with your own unique set of creative abilities given you by God. I trust you will embrace the task of creating a new song of worship to the Lord.

Bibliography

Dabaghian, Karen. *A Travelogue of the Interior: Finding Your Voice and God's Heart in the Psalms*. Colorado Springs, CO: David C. Cook Publishing, 2014.

Freedman, David Noel. *Psalm 119: The Exaltation of Torah*. Vol 6 of *Biblical and Judaic Studies*. Edited by William Henry Propp. Winona Lake, IN: Eisenbrauns, 1999.

Kitchen, John. *Life as Worship: When Reverence Defines Reality*. Fort Washington, PA: CLC Publications, 2015.

Lock, Anne Vaughan. *The Collected Works of Anne Vaughan Lock*. Edited by Susan M. Felch. Vol. 185 of *Medieval & Renaissance Texts & Studies*. Tempe, AZ: Renaissance English Text Society, 1999.

Locke, Anne. *A Meditation of a Penitent Sinner*. Edited by Kel Morin-Parsons. Waterloo, Ontario: North Waterloo Academic Press, 1997.

Longman III, Tremper. *How to Read the Psalms*. Downers Grove, IL: Inter Varsity Press, 1988.

MacDonald, George. *Diary of an Old Soul*. New York: Barnes and Nobles, Inc., 2006.

Maloney, Les D. *A Word Fitly Spoken: Poetic Artistry in the First Four Acrostics of the Hebrew Psalter*. Vol. 119 of *Studies in Biblical Literature*, edited by Hemchand Gossai. New York: Peter Lang Publishing, 2009.

Sayers, Dorothy L. *The Mind of the Maker*. New York: HarperOne Publishers, 1987.

van Gogh, Vincent. *The Letters of Vincent van Gogh*. Edited by Ronald de Leeuw. Translated by Arnold Pomerans. New York: Penguin Books, 1997.

Waltke, Bruce K., and James M. Houston with Erika Moore. *The Psalms as Christian Worship: A Historical Commentary*. Grand Rapids, MI: William B. Eerdmans Publishing Company, 2010.

Printed in the United States
By Bookmasters